I'm a raving fan of Wendy McKinney. Her warm energy comes through in every line of her new book, *Busy Doing What?* Wendy is passionate about making every moment count in life and wants to inspire you to feel the same. I especially liked her chapter on how to say *no*—so helpful for a people pleaser like me. Your time on Earth is precious—make the most of it! Read *Busy Doing What?* and catch the feeling!"

— Ken Blanchard, coauthor of *The New One Minute Manager*® and *Simple Truths of Leadership*

Everyone has the same 24 hours each day to execute their individual process for success. In *Busy Doing What?* Wendy carefully crafts concepts and tools to help provide you with the motivation and confidence to prioritize and understand what's really important. I enjoyed it tremendously and so will you!

— Stedman Graham, New York Times best-selling author, educator and business advisor.

Motivating, educating, stimulating, and entertaining are just a few words that help describe Wendy McKinney's new book, *Busy Doing What?* Women are often referred to as superwoman and are always busy doing a million things. Busy Doing What suggests that you, the reader, should be busy doing what you love, being a blessing to others and making the world a better place. These concepts are reinforced throughout the colorful chapters. This book will make you laugh as you are uplifted. *Busy Doing What?* affirms that we should be busy getting things done while living our best life. Join the experience. Get your copy today!

— Judge Mablean Ephriam, *Justice with Judge Mablean (JusticeCentral.TV)*

What an AMAZING book! *Busy Doing What?* will have you laughing, crying, learning and yearning for MORE! Tangible and heartfelt tips from a goddess with a heart of gold! Every busy person needs to stop what they're doing this and read this book. Beautiful reminders of what is really important – and what else is just "stuff!" Thank you Wendy for this gift to the world.

— Wendy Urushima-Conn, President & CEO Epilepsy Foundation of San Diego County

If you are ready to get real about managing your priorities and forging a more productive and peaceful life, *Busy Doing What?* is the book for you. Wendy's admonitions, tips, and strategies are simple, convicting, and motivating. This is a resource you'll surely want to share with others.

— Deborah Smith Pegues, Global Speaker/CPA/MBA, Bestselling author of *30 Days to Taming Your Tongue* (over 1.2 million sold) *& Lead Like a Woman*

What Wendy has done with *Busy Doing What?* is pushed us to ask the toughest questions. What and who matters the most to you? Without the answer to those pressing questions, we could spend our time in motion but not on purpose. This book is a clarifying call to live with deeper sincerity. From a sincere heart, many great things are possible.

— Taj Paxton, 5x Emmy Award winning Documentary Producer

This read-worthy inspirational book sparks meaningful reflection and commitment to positive life changing action. It's a fabulous must-read guide to honoring the precious gift of time and completing our life journey with no regrets.

— Dr. Sheryl White, Cultural Psychologist

I wish I had read this book a before I went to college! It is not only genius in its content and richly entertaining but is also timely in response to the greatest threat to mankind's ability to address the escalating number of issues that can only be solved if we learn how to focus, prioritize, and make every moment count.

— Dr. Tracy Payne, Research Faculty and Principal
Investigator, University of South Florida

I loved *Busy Doing What?* I even worked through all the exercises. As someone who has sought treatment for social anxiety and ADHD, the action steps that were created were incredibly similar to the ones given by therapists to help curb procrastination behavior. I believe Wendy's book is a powerful tool in helping people manage and take control of their lives. The participation aspect of the book is key to helping the audience internalize the messaging of the book. I can see groups of people using it as a guidebook and working through it together. I like the way Wendy uses anecdotes and symbolism to help lay people understand the concepts that are being imparted. The writing is warm, and I felt like I was being spoken to by an old friend.

— K. Dixon, Practicing Attorney, Social Justice Advocate

BUSY DOING WHAT?

MAKING EVERY MOMENT COUNT

WENDY L. MCKINNEY

WESTBOW
PRESS®
A DIVISION OF THOMAS NELSON
& ZONDERVAN

WestBow Press books may be ordered through booksellers or by contacting:

WestBow Press
A Division of Thomas Nelson & Zondervan
1663 Liberty Drive
Bloomington, IN 47403
www.westbowpress.com
844-714-3454

ISBN: 978-1-6642-7791-5 (sc)
ISBN: 978-1-6642-7790-8 (hc)
ISBN: 978-1-6642-7789-2 (e)

Library of Congress Control Number: 2022916862

Print information available on the last page.

WestBow Press rev. date: 12/23/2022

I would like to dedicate this book to my two older brothers, Greg and Martin Freeman, my guardian angels who left this earth too soon, in the same year. They both fondly called me "Baby Sister," and I will forever miss their voices. I am so grateful that I was busy living, loving, and laughing with them regularly until they left this Earth.

Contents

Introduction

In the chapters ahead you will be introduced to the many tools and stories that will help you make better decisions on how to best spend your time. I encourage you to read with expectation and anticipation, with the hope that "Busy doing what?" will be a question you will be able to confidently answer. I suggest you read this book with a pen and notebook in hand, allowing you the space to reflect on the "busy steps" at the end of each chapter and engage in answering each question.

Remember that this book is in no way a *one-size-fits-all* solution. Instead, it is intended to take you through a pleasant and joyous journey, through the lives and experiences of others. You will find many examples that may help you discover *your* solution. There may only be one or two points that apply to you, or maybe many more. The most important thing to understand is that you are the only person who can decide what is best and what works for you! It is up to you to determine your best BUSY: believing undeniably that success is yours!

Please be prepared to laugh, cry, scream, and write. Laugh about the things that resonate and are comical. Cry about those areas of frustration that seem insurmountable—until now. Scream when you read and relate to something that calls for outward expression and release. Write your thoughts, desires, and visions as you reflect and ponder.

After completing this book, you will have the tools to live by, the questions to uncover, and the motivation and courage to make wholesale changes in your life. Hopefully, you will finish it with a good idea of what your "busy" should look like and what making every moment count looks like for your life. The shutdown of the 2020 global pandemic really taught us that we can pivot in life if we must. It clearly showed us how we can *stop* everything that we are doing and refocus. We learned that we can own our time and make the best decisions for our future. The shutdown made it clear how valuable time is. During the shutdown many people launched new businesses, wrote books, and created award-winning songs. Some folks reconnected with family, met their children, learned to cook, or started an exercise program. Before the pandemic some of us thought owning our own schedules was impossible.

Over the next several chapters we will explore the journey to finding out how we can have it all, do it all, and see it all and not be *too busy* to enjoy it *all*! Busy doing what? Making every moment count.

Busy Prioritizing

A year from now you will wish you had started today.

—Karen Lamb

Rebecca had an amazing job as an administrative coordinator in a beautiful downtown high-rise. She enjoyed working with highly skilled coworkers and learned a lot along the way. She earned a comfortable income and was good at her job. Actually, she was great at it! Organizing, prioritizing, and using her creativity to improve policies and systems were her strengths, which served the fast-paced organization well. Unfortunately, she worked long hours and had a long commute. She had been working there for over thirteen years and had grown accustomed to the routine, but over time her unhappiness began to outweigh the perks. She hated the long hours, hated the long commute, and hated the job, although she was one of the best.

Rebecca had three small children, and they were growing up fast. After the youngest child was born, she became increasingly resentful about working there until it began to feel unbearable. She wanted to spend more time with her children and husband. So what did Rebecca do? Well, one day she just could not take it anymore and she quit. Yes, she just quit.

In just a few weeks Rebecca began to have the time of her life. She was finally available to spend quality time with her husband and children. She walked her children to school and volunteered in their classrooms to help with crafts and projects, which was her dream. She organized their home using charts and graphs and created weekly schedules for each family member—one of her favorite things to do.

Rebecca was phenomenal at prioritizing. At home she developed a challenging curriculum to help her children improve in the areas in which they struggled. The curriculum consisted of flash cards, fact sheets, and test questions that required additional research and study. She even taught them how to write their most intimate thoughts in their journals to encourage self-reflection. To reinforce the curriculum, Rebecca created an incentive program that was out of this world. The incentive program included gifts and prizes generated by an economic system using tokens. Rebecca's incentive program taught the children how to prioritize and focus. It was one of the most motivating and inspiring programs that I had ever seen designed for children!

Rebecca had a natural sensitivity to children with special needs because one of her sons was diagnosed with autism. As a result, Rebecca started working at the school part-time, helping children with special needs and collaborating with teachers to develop a curriculum to better serve them. She received such positive feedback that she accepted requests from other educational professionals to design programs and activities for students. She would stay up all night designing and building. She finally saw her dreams fulfilled.

Then something terrible happened. Remember how Rebecca had suddenly become so frustrated that she had quit her job?

Remember the great job that had paid so well? Well, her money ran out. Her savings ran out. Rebecca had quit her job out of pure frustration, but she had also quit without a plan. She and her husband had become accustomed to a dual income for over a decade. This sudden change in income became a major stressor and almost devastated their household.

Rebecca and I had a chance to connect over our favorite Starbucks drink. She told me she was becoming depressed and frustrated because her financial situation was taking a toll on her. She was ready to quit again and go back to work. Her perfect scenario had become her worst nightmare. She began to doubt her decision to leave her great-paying job. She blamed herself for jumping too quickly without a clear plan. How was it possible for Rebecca to be miserable, depressed, and running out of money while doing what she loved most?

I thought about Rebecca early one morning in my quiet time of meditation. Suddenly, the ideas came like a mighty, rushing wind. I sent her text after text with the ideas that were pouring in my mind for her. The revelation I received was that she needed to *prioritize* monetizing her passion. She needed to figure out how to *turn her passion into provision* for her family. She needed a plan.

It was clear that her skills, talent, and creativity was in high demand. So many parents needed help with their children's education, organization, and behavior. I suggested the idea of creating a business called Mother's Helper, where she would provide after-school care for a small number of children, right in her home. This wouldn't be your typical after-school care program with Goldfish crackers and Nickelodeon videos but after-school care accompanied by Rebecca's uniquely customized curriculum

3

and incentive program. The craziest thing was that she had been thinking of this idea for a while but did not quite know where to start.

We began discussing business planning, acquiring the appropriate licensing, and collaborating with the teachers, principals, and staff. She shared her ideas with other parents at her kids' school. The interest was beyond her expectation. Well, the rest is history, and Rebecca was able to follow her dream. After spending time with Rebecca and helping her discover the idea to monetize her dream, I soon realized that you *can* have what you want. You *can* do what you want. You *can* wake up every day and do what you love. You *can* inspire and enhance lives while providing an income for you and your family. You *can* be fulfilled and fed! You *can* follow your dreams.

We soon found out that Rebecca had many other creative talents that she loved and enjoyed that could also be monetized, giving her many streams of income. She was even able to create a product line of educational materials and crafts that she could sell all over the world. She began to work long hours and enjoyed every moment. She was able to spend time with her children and her family and change lives all at the same time, without missing a beat. She became increasingly busy, but this time around, she was busy making every moment count!

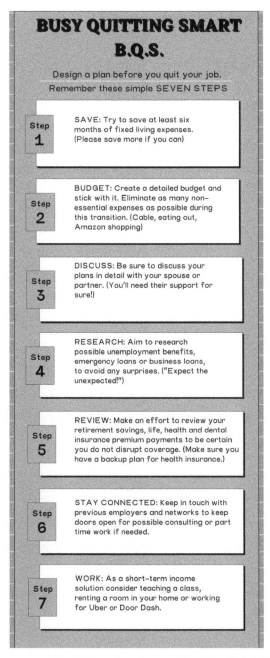

BUSY QUITTING SMART

B.Q.S.

Design a plan before you quit your job.
Remember these simple SEVEN STEPS

Step 1
SAVE: Try to save at least six months of fixed living expenses. (Please save more if you can)

Step 2
BUDGET: Create a detailed budget and stick with it. Eliminate as many non-essential expenses as possible during this transition. (Cable, eating out, Amazon shopping)

Step 3
DISCUSS: Be sure to discuss your plans in detail with your spouse or partner. (You'll need their support for sure!)

Step 4
RESEARCH: Aim to research possible unemployment benefits, emergency loans or business loans, to avoid any surprises. ("Expect the unexpected!")

Step 5
REVIEW: Make an effort to review your retirement savings, life, health and dental insurance premium payments to be certain you do not disrupt coverage. (Make sure you have a backup plan for health insurance.)

Step 6
STAY CONNECTED: Keep in touch with previous employers and networks to keep doors open for possible consulting or part time work if needed.

Step 7
WORK: As a short-term income solution consider teaching a class, renting a room in your home or working for Uber or Door Dash.

Picture created in 2022 and authorized by Wendy McKinney.

Time for Busy Steps!

Busy Prioritizing

Questions and Self-Reflection

1. What is something that you have always loved doing or wanted to do but did not have the time, money, or motivation to execute?

   _____

   _____

   _____

   _____

   _____

   _____

   _____

2. Can you identify someone in your life who is (or was) doing something that you would like to do? What are they doing? How are they doing it?

   _____

   _____

   _____

   _____

   _____

   _____

   _____

3. What does success look like for them? For you? Please explain.

_____

_____

_____

_____

_____

_____

_____

4. Please write down one or two areas of interest or ideas that you might want to prioritize and monetize.

_____

_____

_____

_____

_____

_____

_____

Busy Defining
What's Really Important

Vision without action is a Daydream.
Action without vision is a Nightmare.

—Japanese proverb

M y brother Jeffery received two master's degrees back to back, one in business and one in engineering. For about four years we did not see him at any activities, events, or family functions. He followed his dream and accomplished his goal in record time. He was able to secure a promotion at his job and explore many different avenues in life. On the other hand, what about the things he missed? What about the sacrifices he made? How important were they compared to obtaining his degrees? Did he make every moment count?

Well, let's address those questions and give them some thought. Let's take two people who have a desire to return to school to complete their degrees (like Jeffery did) and examine the decisions of Student A and Student B. We will call Student A Adam and Student B Brian.

Adam buckled down and focused completely on school, like my brother Jeffery. Adam canceled all extracurricular activities and family outings. Yes, *all,* including family reunions, concerts, birthday parties, art shows, and weekend getaways. Two years later Adam received his degree and had positioned himself for new goals, ventures, and opportunities. Adam now had the flexibility to choose the life he wanted and start the career or business he had dreamed about. Obtaining a degree was important to Adam, so that was his priority and the choice he made.

Now we will examine Brian's decisions. Brian decided to put off finishing college because he felt like he had other pressing priorities. He was in a new relationship. He wanted to travel and had a few weddings he had been invited to attend. He also wanted to pay off old debts before going back to school.

He wasn't sure what he wanted his major to be and he did not invest much time into figuring it out. Additionally, he would always get frustrated with the financial aid paperwork and process. That alone was enough to put off completing it. Brian figured he could always go to school again sometime in the near future. Was Brian just thinking of all the excuses in the world to avoid going back to college? Did he consider that making these other choices could potentially be detrimental to his future?

Brian lost two years that he could have spent completing school. We know it was Brian's goal to complete school, and he needed a college degree to advance in his field. Those two years were gone forever, and Brian might have missed out on opportunities that he desired. He might have missed out on a promotion at his job or a huge contract for his new business.

Although those years were gone, there was still hope for Brian. Now was the time to make every moment count. Brian must count the costs and reexamine his priorities. It was time to press reset and pick up where he had left off. He could use his experience as a learning opportunity to do everything in his power to get back on track, refocus, and reach his goal.

There are many roadblocks to accomplishing our goals. Everyone may not be as disciplined as Adam and my brother Jeffery. You might need to create strategies to help complete your goals. You might need a coach or an accountability partner. It really is OK to reach out for help. Some people are better at completing their short- and long-term goals without support. Then there are some of us who almost need a drill sergeant to scream at us and threaten us until we get it done. We will explore more tips and tricks throughout the book that might help.

You might have several distractions in your life. You might not be sure of your goals and dreams and are trying to make discoveries. What is most important is that you self-examine and execute. Try not to keep putting your hopes and dreams off until later because later is not promised. Define your priorities and set balance. You can enjoy friends and family at the appropriate times, but sacrifices must be made when there is a goal in mind. It hurts, but sometimes you have to be selfish with your time. There might be circumstances beyond your control that force you to make the difficult decision to put your goals and dreams on hold. If you can strategize, make it happen. By any means necessary, develop a plan and stick to it. Life is short and we want to make every moment count!

A suggestion for balance would be to find a way to incorporate the activities of your goals into time spent with family and friends. For example, Denise, a friend of mine, was working on her PhD dissertation. Denise would need to commit literally hundreds of hours to reaching this goal. Instead of completely isolating all her friends and family for weeks, months, or years, she got creative and incorporated them into her research. Dinners, parties, and family events became dual-focused, filled with fun and function. She had her family and friends complete surveys, participate in interviews, create topics and content, and so much more. Denise's friends and family felt like they were contributing to her success— and they were indeed. Denise was able to stay engaged, connected, and on pace to reach her goal without ever neglecting the ones she cared about most. Of course, there were times when Denise needed to buckle down by herself and focus, but she was creative and found a way to make every moment count.

How did this story end? Denise, very successfully, reached her goal and was awarded her PhD. Today Denise is an executive coach and helps others overcome obstacles and reach their goals. Denise was super busy but made every moment count and committed to a life of helping others. Denise got busy doing everything she could by defining what was really important and getting it done!

Time for Busy Steps!

Busy Defining What's Really Important

Questions & Self-Reflection

1. What are some things in your life that are important to you that you might be neglecting?

   _____

   _____

   _____

   _____

   _____

2. Does your personal story sound more like Adam's or Brian's? How so?

   _____

   _____

   _____

   _____

   _____

3. If your personal story sounds more like Adam's, explain how you will remain focused on what's important to you and how you might be able to help others do the same.

   _____

   _____

   _____

   _____

   _____

4. If your personal story sounds more like Brian's, what are three things in your life that are preventing you from focusing on what is important?

_____

_____

_____

_____

_____

5. Can you identify a "Denise" in your life who can coach you and keep you focused on the things that are really important? Explain how, and designate when you will approach them.

_____

_____

_____

_____

_____

Busy Avoiding Distractions

Distraction is the great destroyer of dreams.
Why be busy being busy when you were built to
inspire the world!

—Robin Sharma

W hat is the opposite of being focused? *Doing everything except what you should be doing!* Doing things that get in the way of your greatness. Watching what others are doing. Being busy doing everything except making every moment count. The opposite of being focused is to be *busy* being *distracted*! As we explore the action of being BUSY—believing undeniably that success is yours—let's discuss a concept called distraction addiction.

Distraction Addiction Defined

Distraction addictions can keep you from progress, purpose, and prosperity. Distraction addictions can keep you from happiness, joy, and peace. These distraction addictions speak to you and tell you that you *need* them and there is no other way! They tell you that this is the best choice for now, and they can end up deceiving you for a lifetime.

Distraction is something that prevents someone from giving full attention to something else. To be *distracted* is to have your focus interrupted, sometimes briefly and sometimes often. For example, receiving a social media notification in the middle of reading an important email and stopping to read it. Another example is the constant interruption or distraction of the notifications on an Apple Watch. (It drives me crazy when I am trying to have a conversation with someone and they keep glancing at their smart watch every few seconds.)

Addiction occurs when someone has a strong inclination to do, use, or indulge in something repeatedly, at any cost. An *addiction* is an urge to do something that is hard to control or stop. Some common examples, of course, might include addiction to prescription drugs, excessive alcohol, tobacco, food, or sex. A less common example of addiction, although it occurs quite frequently, might be an addiction to staying in a relationship that is absolutely fruitless because you are addicted to having someone in your life and hate the thought of being by yourself.

Another example of addiction that we will explore is staying in a job that you hate, for years and years, simply because you are addicted to the money and you think this is as good as it gets. You might think this income level is as high as you can get when you are just over broke (JOB). Although there are other opportunities or jobs available, you cannot seem to tear yourself away from this one that you hate.

Distraction Addiction: Impossibilities

When you put *distraction* and *addiction* together, you create an atmosphere of impossibilities. *When you are distracted, it is almost impossible for you to start. When you are addicted, it is almost impossible for you to stop.* Distraction addiction can keep you from starting something that would be greatly beneficial to you because you cannot let go of what is potentially harmful to you.

Distraction addiction can often be subtle and hard to detect. The distraction or addiction component is usually something enjoyable but may not be the best for you at that particular time. You can get caught up in a vicious cycle that can be difficult to terminate.

Distraction addiction is the inability to stop or control the urge to yield to the interruption of the activity, project, or area of focus. Distraction addiction can be irritating and disruptive, but you just can't seem to stop. It has become a part of you. It has become a part of your regular behavior. It can become a regular part of your character if you are not careful. Distraction addiction can occur when you are caught up in a revolving loop and can't detach. Distraction addiction is almost like listening to a music track that gets stuck on one word and keeps repeating until you want to throw the entire music player out the window.

Distraction addiction is lying in the bed, hour after hour, watching shows on Netflix, one after another, knowing that you have so many more important and productive things to do like exercise, meal prep, finish that book, write that song, or submit that proposal. However, you just cannot seem to muster the strength to pick up the remote and turn off the TV. Emails and social media interruptions can also take you for an eternal ride on the distraction addiction procrastination highway!

Distraction addiction can be brief, or it can last a lifetime, permanently keeping you from your purpose and greatest accomplishments. It can keep you returning to that activity, thing, or person that is taking you away from your primary goal.

Distraction addiction can allow you to get close to your goals or to fulfilling your purpose, but it will *never* allow you to reach your goals. Distraction addiction can be devastating and can deliver you into a vicious cycle of repeated failures if you are not careful. The reasons and results can be numerous. Let us review five common examples of the consequences of distraction addiction.

Consequences

1. Missing out on a promotion or job opportunity.
2. Helping someone else fulfill their dreams while neglecting your own. (It is often easier to follow someone else's greatness rather than be responsible for your own.)
3. Ruining a relationship because of neglect or abandonment.
4. Experiencing declining health because of a conflicting commitment.
5. Losing a business opportunity as a result of preoccupation or disconnection.

Fear Factor

Why can't I focus? Why am I so distracted? FEAR: false evidence appearing real. Often, distraction addiction grabs hold of you because you have somehow been forced to believe that this is the best you can do for yourself, or you are convinced that this is as good as it gets. You have been fooled by fear, or your confidence has been crushed by someone or something. Distraction addiction can completely consume you and cause you to essentially lose hope.

Zig Ziglar said that FEAR has two meanings. The choice is yours to make: Either you "forget everything and run" or "face everything and rise."

Symptoms

Let's explore four common symptoms of distraction addiction, plus the mama of them all.

1. You are constantly laser-focused on the execution of multiple projects that belong to someone else while neglecting several major projects of your own.
2. You find yourself getting involved in the most ridiculous, unnecessary, and inconsequential activities at the same time you have extremely important personal deadlines.
3. You find every unreasonable excuse to do everything under the sun except for the necessary tasks at hand. You, of course, find things to do that are fun, playful, and exciting, which helps time to pass so quickly.
4. You find yourself feeling terrified at the thought of starting a project or activity and you create preliminary projects, convincing yourself of their importance to your progress.

Here is a very simple example:

You have a serious case of distraction addiction when you find yourself pausing to get a snack, when you go to the refrigerator, only to forget about the snack and take this precious time to throw out all of the expired food from the refrigerator. Next you find yourself reorganizing the condiments and placing them in plastic containers. While immersed in this task, you then feel compelled to match the plastic containers with their appropriate fitted lids and matching colors. Of course, now you will have to complete this burst of organizing by wiping the glass shelves in the refrigerator with disinfectant, not realizing that you have wasted an hour because of chronic distraction addiction. You could have come much closer to progress or completion of that very necessary project, if only you would have stayed focused!

The "One More Thing" Syndrome

The mama of the distraction addiction symptoms is the "one more thing" syndrome. Every time you prepare yourself to sit down and start that very important task or activity, you suddenly realize that there is *one more thing* that you must absolutely do before you get started. You have convinced yourself that this *one more thing* will significantly contribute to the imminent success of your world-changing project, only to discover that one more thing turns into two more things, then three more things, until you realize that you never got started on the project and it has become impossible to stay focused. You never reach your goal. Minutes turn into hours. Hours turn into days. Days turn into weeks, months, and then years. Before you know it, you have completely abandoned your project and your goal.

One more thing can also include checking emails, responding to text messages, and taking a sneak peek at the latest Facebook, Instagram, and Twitter posts. Please do not forget about those very important videos you need to watch. Oh yes! The videos are on auto play, so you will need to watch a few of them until you see one that isn't as interesting or relevant.

From what I have heard—because I personally would never fall for the "one more thing" syndrome (it's really one of my worst habits)—this can become an extremely difficult habit to break, and it can devastate your success. Here are a few quick tools and suggestions that you can grasp while working through these challenges.

Tools

Take advantage of the timers on your phone. To start, set your timer for thirty minutes, then get to work. If the presence of your phone becomes a distraction, you might need to place it in a separate room to help you accomplish the designated task.

Focus on one task at a time. See it to completion, nonstop, uninterrupted, until you hear the sound of the timer. If you are really in the groove, simply hit repeat and keep at it for another thirty minutes. If you need a break, by all means, please take a break. Make sure it is a timed break. Taking breaks can help you to become more productive. A ten- to fifteen-minute break would be my suggestion. Take a walk, call a friend, grab some coffee, then get back to work.

Distractions destroy action. If it's not moving
you towards your purpose, leave it alone!
—Jermaine Riley

The Cure

Enough already! I can't take it! *Help!* This feels like some type
of disease, and we need to find a cure. What is the *cure* for this
disastrous disease called distraction addiction?

Here are seven remedies to consider. These seven steps may
not provide a cure for every facet of the disease, but they will
certainly help get you started on your journey to success.

1. Turn on your automated "why" notifications
2. What if?
3. The plan
4. Meditation and visualization
5. Simplify! Simplify! Simplify!
6. Accountability partner(s)
7. Eliminate, don't procrastinate!

1. Turn On Your Automated "Why" Notifications

Have you defined your "why" lately? Why do you want to
change your situation? Why do you feel the need to do something
different? Why aren't you satisfied with the decisions you have
made? Why do you want to complete that project or proposal?

Let's make an attempt to cure this distraction addiction
disease by activating your automated "why" notifications. Let's set
them to alert you, and be ready to launch at all times. It would also

be great to create built-in defenses and backup built-in defenses to help you overcome these challenges of distraction addiction. If you are anything like me, you know how to self-manipulate or deceive yourself into believing that the distraction addiction you are experiencing is not so bad, that it will get better, or that it's only temporary. I hate to inform you, but those are all lies! Please! Please! Please be honest and truthful with yourself! You won't regret it!

Example notifications reminding you of your "why" might be a photo of a family member who passed away who had encouraged you or motivated you. Maybe you have notifications that contain a quote or a song that stimulates and inspires you to get moving and get things done. Maybe you have a notification of your reasons why you want to be happy, healthy, and whole! You decide. If you stop and allow the thoughts to flow, your reasons why will surface and you will be reminded of your greatness at every turn. How can you lose when you know "why"? There is very little room for distraction addiction when you are constantly reminded of your "why"!

2. What If?

Another suggested remedy that can possibly help cure the dreadful distraction addiction disease is to create "what if" statements surrounding your goal. These statements should remain clearly visible and should be quickly accessible on your phone, posted at eye level around your house, or boldly displayed at your job or in your car. "What if" additionally represents "What would/could/should happen if …?"

Here are a few examples:

- What if I completed my book and it became a best seller?
- What if I quit my job and got a better one?
- What if a producer heard my music and decided to sign me for a record deal?
- What if I found the love of my life after terminating a very toxic relationship?
- What if I stopped complaining and started focusing on the good and the great?
- What if I stuck with a new workout plan and lost thirty pounds?
- What if my life changed for the better if I made some serious decisions?

Positive answers to these questions could be life-changing. Focusing on these answers might help you concentrate and execute.

Creating and displaying these statements helps to bring you fully into the present moment when you need to be productive and engaged. When your attention is geared toward moving forward and progressing, distraction addiction can dissipate and potentially disappear. Creativity is automatically stimulated. Ideas, thoughts, and concepts begin to flow effortlessly. There's no room for distraction addiction. You've got work to do! The world is waiting on you. It is time to soar!

3. The Plan

A plan. A schedule. Long term and short term. How much more should we say here? You get the picture. You know the drill. Benjamin Franklin said, "Fail to plan or you will plan to fail!" The successful pilot and poet Antoine de Saint–Exupéry reminded us that "A goal without a plan is a wish!" Plan! Plan! Plan some more! You can use the planning template in the next chapter. Keep your plans nearby on your nightstand, at your desk, in your car, in the bathroom, or anywhere you might experience distraction addiction. It's like laying mouse traps around the house. Instead, you are laying the most efficiently written plans around your environment and catching success and measurable progress. A suggestion would be to become familiar with digital planning tools and web-based applications. It will be like laying distraction addiction traps at every turn. Let's get it done!

4. Meditation and Visualization

The living, breathing, moving, vision board. Visualize what your life would be like when you finished that book, song, proposal, or project. Meditate on how your life would be if you were able to move on from that hindering job or deteriorating relationship that has kept you from fulfilling your purpose. What joy would it bring? Can you picture it? Can you visualize it? Who else would benefit other than you? How will you affect those around you? How will you change the world?

Meditating and visualizing the outcome that you desire can bring life and manifestation of your dreams and goals. Vision boards have become a very popular and useful tool over the years to help people visualize their dreams, but what about a living, breathing, moving vision board? Please allow me to explain. While struggling to write this book, two of my dear friends gave me the best birthday present ever. It was the birthday present of a lifetime! They wanted to provide me with an environment and atmosphere that would help me get to the finish line for writing this book. They created what I call a living, breathing, moving, vision board.

This is how they pulled it off. Valerie and Ashley took all of the furniture out of Valerie's house and converted Valerie's home into an actual book-writing station. When I arrived at the front door, I had no idea what they were up to. They mysteriously escorted me down the visualization highway. When I first entered the house there were signs everywhere with the title of my book. It looked so real. Then we walked into the next room which was decorated as the book's launch party with real invitations, red carpet, champagne, and balloons everywhere. It was amazing! I laughed and I cried. Most importantly, I was in the moment, and I could imagine a real, live book launch party.

The next room was set up as the book-signing event with a table, business cards displaying my book title and headshot, and actual books covered with a graphic of my book title (which were children's books from Valerie's personal library, wrapped with my book cover). Also featured was a Sharpie marker and a chair, staged and ready for me to share my autograph with my new readers as they lined up to purchase their books.

The third room was set up with a series of chairs arranged theater-style to resemble an audience, and a make-believe stage and backdrop that had been made from black plastic tablecloths taped to the walls. Positioned on the black wall was the official TED Talks logo. The resemblance of an authentic TED Talks stage was frightening but exhilarating at the same time. Presenting at a TED Talk has always been my dream. There were more tears as I imagined and visualized the crowd roaring and my book actually being published, promoted, and sold.

Next they led me upstairs into the book-writing closet. All over the walls were quotes about the importance and significance of finishing the book. A large portion of the previously hanging clothes and contents of the closet had been removed for this area of visualization as well. I was overwhelmed, excited, and anxious, but I eagerly welcomed this productive space.

There were notepads, my favorite snacks, and alkaline water to keep me energized and supplied with everything I would need to keep writing. Finally, they told me to have a seat, get comfortable, and turn on the two oversized monitors. Suddenly, in Dolby stereo surround sound, I heard my husband's voice and his face appeared with an encouraging message, along with a dozen other personalized motivational videos from my family members and dear friends. Each person was encouraging me to finish the book and reminding me of how important it was to them and to me. I couldn't stop the tears from flowing. I stayed in that closet for about seventeen hours! I was so motivated and pumped! It was the best experience ever. I cried and typed. I laughed and typed. I got inspired and typed. I dreamed and typed. I visualized and typed some more.

This activity for meditation and visualization is extreme, but it was quite effective. Valerie and Ashley's exercise helped me live in the moment of completion and execution. I was able to see and feel what it would be like to bring this baby to life, and it felt good. Side note: another significant motivator was that I did not want to let the ladies down, not even for one second, since they had gone through so much trouble to bring the vision to life.

I encourage you to bring your vision to life, or ask two of your best friends to help you. Whether it's an attempt to start a business, finish a book, a song, or a proposal or whether it is the desire to end a relationship or quit a job, this exercise can—and will—help you stay focused and motivated. This exercise can help heal you from the compelling forces of distraction addiction.

I was so full of inspiration that I was not easily distracted at all. I was fully engaged. All I wanted to do was get closer to completion. Not just in that moment, but every time I would sit down to write or even think about writing, I remained focused.

5. Simplify! Simplify! Simplify!

Distraction addiction can quickly surface when you are overloaded. Have you considered simplifying your life so that you avoid becoming overwhelmed and frustrated and can't process clearly? Oftentimes we can't think straight because we are on activity overload. It's perfectly fine to be highly productive, and even busy. Busy doing what? When on activity overload, we tend to make bad choices and poor decisions. This can easily cause us to slip into the distraction addiction mode if we are not careful. Erratically juggling multiple projects, competing relationships, stressful diets, and the vicissitudes of life can earn you the profile of a confused circus clown. Some people can manage and can win an award for the best multitasker in the world, while others crumble every time.

Nonetheless, if your life is simplified, as much as you can possibly simplify it, you allow room for clarity and creativity instead of stress and depression. Simplifying—or better yet, streamlining—your life can provide you with some of the best benefits that money can buy. You will see improvements in your health and relationships. You will see progress in your goals. You will experience better responses when communicating. You just might experience a cure for distraction addiction.

6. Accountability Partner(s)

This is a good one. This is a great remedy for curing distraction addiction. Imagine that you are about to enter a potentially endless state of a Netflix coma and your accountability partner gives you a call. You would have been saved by the bell. Without that accountability partner, you might have fallen into a complete Netflix abyss, never to rise again. Thank goodness you have made a commitment to this accountability partner to stick with the plan, allowing him or her to rattle your world and get you back on track. Some people need this regularly, while others don't need it at all. However, if you suffer from distraction addiction disease or even minor traces of it, accountability must become a permanent part of your process.

The accountability remedy for curing distraction addiction disease includes reaching out and consulting with a counselor, therapist, coach, or a good friend to solicit help and support on how to push through this bottleneck that's keeping you from progress. It might be best to schedule sessions and create an accountability plan. The plan should be very specific, measurable, achievable, relevant, and time-sensitive.[1] There should be a sense of urgency built around the plan. It's very important that you follow through and try your best to be consistent. Be accountable. Make a commitment.

Everyone needs support as they are approaching progress and potentially running into speed bumps along the road. Michael Jordan always had a coach. Serena Williams never let a day go by without working with a coach. World-renowned speaker, coach, and best-selling author Tony Robbins coaches presidents, athletes, and royalty. Most of the world's greatest leaders have coaches. Their coach is someone they can trust, lean on, and can be accountable to, someone who can help eliminate those constant visits from the distraction addiction monster, someone who can help get them on track and help remove the fogginess that is blocking their goal. There are coaches that are accessible all over the world. You will have to do your homework to find the best one that will work for you. I promise that they are only a phone call, an email, or a Google search away. Please do not wait too long or the distraction addiction monster will be at your heels! Some individuals might need a team of coaches if the distraction addiction is often recurring. You will have to self-evaluate and get to work.

7. Eliminate, Don't Procrastinate!

As mentioned above, distraction addiction can be mitigated by implementing the process of simplifying and creating plans and notifications. Another more direct approach is to, quite frankly, introduce the idea to *eliminate*. If Netflix is holding you back from success, temporarily discontinue your membership. Eliminate! If you have a job where transition opportunities seem momentarily unattainable, start volunteering at places where you have an interest. This provides a more goal-oriented environment and can help start the transition process from that job. One time, when I was ready to move on to another job opportunity, I cleaned out my office completely as if I was leaving. I removed every photo from my desk. I boxed up and took home every personal item. I removed every photo and award that had been hanging on the walls until they were completely bare. Every time I walked into that office I was reminded that it was time to move on. I was reminded that it was time to put my strategic exit plan in place—and I did.

You can start your plan to cut ties as soon as possible. Eliminate! If it is a relationship that you need to get out of, get *busy* and get super involved in projects and activities that fuel your purpose. Hopefully, you will begin to enjoy the life that is absent of that burdensome relationship and start making concrete plans to move on. Eliminate! Make sure that you begin to move away from the relationship and not closer to it. If fear and doubt exist, it's time to eliminate and replace them with courage and confidence.

Sometimes moving forward requires moving forward amid fear. If you want to swim in your pool and the water is cold, eliminate the fear and jump in, feet first. All fear is gone, and the distraction addiction doors are closed behind you.

Get into the habit of asking yourself. Does this
support the life I am trying to create?
—Irisa Yardenah

Wendy L. McKinney

Time for Busy Steps!

Busy Avoiding Distractions

Questions & Self-Reflection

1. Name one distraction addiction that you struggle with.

   _____
   _____
   _____
   _____
   _____

2. Can you think of a time when you suffered from the "one more thing" syndrome? How did it affect your day?

   _____
   _____
   _____
   _____
   _____

3. What is the best course of action to help you recover? Choose one action from the seven cures.

   _____
   _____
   _____
   _____
   _____

Busy Giving All You've Got

Then Fall Out and Rest Easy!

> Inaction breeds doubt and fear. Action breeds confidence and courage. If you want to conquer fear, do not sit home and think about it. Go out and get busy!
>
> —Dale Carnegie

Every day is a *race*! Your goal should be to make every effort to get through the race every day, giving it your best. Give it all you've got and make sure you are doing what you love or are walking in your purpose. Run hard but do what aligns best with your purpose! Remember to balance and work smart each day, trying to make the best use of your time with every moment ... then fall out at the end of the day and rest easy! Go to bed early and wake up bright and early, ready to start this journey of success all over again. My mother would tell us the first thing we should do is slide right onto our knees as soon as we wake up, before we get going in the morning. Make time for devotion, meditation, and prayer. Hear from your higher power on what the direction is for your life today. Sarah Young's *Jesus Calling* is an excellent daily devotional designed to guide you with insight and reflection, leading to powerful revelation to help you through the anticipation of the day. There are many devotionals available. Please choose one that is best suited for you. Next, eat a healthy breakfast, put your "running shoes" on, and get in position for greatness!

Now, remember, you do not have to win the race. All you need to do is finish. Your primary goal should be to achieve your personal best. *Just finish*! You do not have to measure your pace or speed against anyone else's. You do not know or understand their circumstances, regardless of what you see or what they may tell you. You do not necessarily understand the details of their situation, their history, or their current challenges. My Aunt Mablean often says, "You don't know the story behind all the glory!" All you know is your own story. All you know is *you* ... so *do you*!

Twenty-Four Hours

> Lack of direction, not lack of time, is the problem.
> We all have twenty-four-hour days.
> —Zig Ziglar

Time is so precious. Each day we only have a small amount of time to do everything. I used to wish and hope I could figure out how to avoid sleeping to give myself more hours in the day to work on projects. It never worked out because I would be dog-tired the next week as my body tried to rebuild and recover what I had stolen from it. The result would end up being a full week of exhaustion and less productivity. It is better to just go to bed. You will feel so much better. We will explore more of that later in this chapter.

Let's take a look at how much time we have in a day. What does your typical day look like? Every day we typically:

1. Sleep
2. Eat
3. Bathe
4. Use the bathroom
5. Work
6. Talk on the phone
7. Email
8. Text
9. Check social media
10. Commute
11. Walk/run
12. Exercise
13. Relax
14. Open mail
15. Clean up/organize
16. Read/study
17. Pay bills
18. Participate in spiritual practice (go to church, pray, meditate)
19. Spend time with family and friends
20. Run errands
21. Perform beauty routines
22. Shop

How can we do all these things every day in twenty-four hours? On a weekday we typically work about eight to ten hours, sleep six to eight hours, and spend at least two or three hours to eat. Some of us might commute one to two hours, meaning we spend about seventeen to twenty-three hours carrying out regular activities, leaving us just a few hours (depending on your circumstances, of course) to do whatever we want. You must make a choice. Making every moment count is a decision. It is always and only your decision.

The world-changing shutdown of the 2020 global pandemic forced us to make true behavioral shifts and taught us the true value of time. Being required to stay home for days, weeks, and even months at a time forced most of us to seriously evaluate what was really important. Suddenly, everyone had more time than ever. No more excuses about commuting issues and traffic jams, because most everyone was working from home, on their laptops and in their pajamas. Meetings via video conferencing hit an all-time high. Some people found themselves lost with this new gift of time, while others took advantage and connected with family, started new businesses, and instituted true self-care. It's up to you to decide how you want to spend your time. Everyone has the same twenty-four hours to do whatever they want.

At the end of the day, you might want to ask yourself a few questions. *What am I trying to accomplish? What am I busy doing? Am I really making every moment count?*

It is amazing how busy we say we are, but somehow we find the time to binge-watch seventy-three episodes of a popular TV series. That is seventy-three hours of screen time. Talk about being busy! Clearly, we might say we are busy, but we essentially make time for what we want.

This book is primarily written for those of us who struggle with being super busy, doing a lot of something or maybe a lot of nothing. However, some are not quite fulfilled with the current situations in their lives. Are we afraid we will miss something or run out of "life" before we finish? With your best effort, how can you best affect change and leave this world better than you found it?

As a side note, if you are stuck trying to figure out your passion and purpose, there are behavioral evaluation tests and discover-your-gift tests that might help you streamline your interests. There is so much to do in the world, but we must choose. There is the Myers-Briggs test, StrengthsFinder, and many more. You can also try Googling "How to discover my passion or gifts"!

This is one of my favorite poems about the consumption of time. I would hear my father-in-law quote it often:

"One Minute," Dr. Benjamin E. Mays

I have only just a minute,
Only sixty seconds in it.
Forced upon me, can't refuse it.
Didn't seek it, didn't choose it.
But it's up to me
to use it.
Just a tiny little minute,
But eternity is in it.

This poem reminds me of the importance of every single minute. Once it is gone, it is gone forever. "But eternity is in it." It's my choice to do something great or gamble it away, hoping that I get another chance. The best part for me is "but it's up to me to use it." I am energized and reminded that I have the power to make my own decision to make every moment count.

Your Personal Best

Unfortunately, so many of us make the decision to quit or give up when we feel like we can't offer our personal best. Often, we feel inadequate or undervalued. We might start on something until the voices creep in. These voices tell us that we are not good enough, smart enough, experienced enough, or perfect enough. Eventually, we self-sabotage or make millions of excuses for why we haven't followed through.

Your personal best means just that, doing the best that you can do. You can't do any better than that. Five-time Olympic gold medalist Simone Biles said, "A successful competition for me is always going out there and putting 100 percent into whatever I'm doing. It's not always winning. People, I think, mistake that it's just winning. Sometimes it could be, but for me, it's hitting the best sets I can, gaining confidence, and having a good time and having fun."

The secret is to find that target. Where is the finish line for your personal best? For starters, you cannot measure your personal best according to someone else's measuring stick. You must design a stick of your own. Other people think that they are the best at educating you on what's best for you when their true concern should be focusing on their own successes and challenges.

Speaking of successes and challenges and giving your personal best, my husband strongly suggested that I invest in an Apple Watch because he felt like it would help me keep better track of my exercise and help motivate me to stay on task. I resisted for months because I felt like the watch was invasive and outright creepy in the way it would track my every move and even my lack of movement. Go figure! I firmly believed that I was doing just fine without it and manual tracking would offer great results as well. My husband was a total Apple Watch advocate. He wore his watch every day, and even throughout the night if he had enough of a charge. Did you know it can measure your breathing and sleep patterns? Super creepy.

Regardless of my continued resistance, when my birthday came in February, he bought one for me anyway. I reluctantly accepted the gift and now I am embarrassingly addicted.

The Apple Watch has three rings that measure your activity for the day. One ring measures how many times you stand each hour. Another ring measures how long you have exercised consistently for the day. The final ring measures all your movements for the day based on calories burned. That last one is called your "moves" ring.

For weeks I was measuring how many calories I was burning against my husband's and my cousin Autumn's caloric measurements. For the life of me, I couldn't understand how I could exercise for longer periods than both of them but still burn fewer calories.

Well, after further research, I discovered that the output of the results for each ring is measured differently for each person because of their body weight, strength, movement, speed, etc. Just like in real life, so many personal factors are used to measure success that you just can't compare yourself to others. Well, you can, but it is pointless. I believe the best way to create the measurement for your personal best is to set reasonable goals, track your accomplishments, and adjust your goals accordingly. You— and no one else—own the rights to the measuring tape or the finish line of your life. If you can embrace this concept, you will win every time. You will win every time against yourself, which is all that really matters. That is your personal best.

What's most important is that you keep moving, keep striving, and keep progressing toward a greater goal. Before you know it, you will surpass your greatest dreams in many areas of your life.

A friend of mine decided that she wanted to go back to school and obtain her bachelor's degree after working a full-time job for many years. She decided to take baby steps, applied to a university, got accepted, started taking a few classes at a time. Before she knew it, she was walking across that stage in her polyester gown, jamming to "Pomp and Circumstance"! She was a married woman and a mother who worked a full-time job. She had not been to school in over a decade. No excuses. She set a goal and kept it going. She didn't compete with anyone except herself. As a matter of fact, she didn't tell many people that she was in school. This helped her to focus and not allow outside chatter to discourage her or *distract* her. She kept her own pace but made sure she kept *busy* moving forward. This focus helped her develop a rhythm for success!

She kept it going. Soon after, she quickly enrolled in a certification program and got *busy* and became a certified life coach in a very short period. Next, she was so motivated and inspired that she applied for the master's program. Again, in just a few years she had obtained her master's degree. These accomplishments afforded her the opportunity to advance in her career, accept promotions, and change jobs for better opportunities. As a matter of fact, after several years she was actually recruited back to an organization where she had worked previously. They offered her a position for which she would have never qualified had she not advanced in her educational goals. This was all because she gave her personal best.

She was having lunch one day in the lunchroom (at her new job that was once her old job) when one of her coworkers sat down and joined her for lunch. This young lady had worked in the same position with my friend before she left several years prior. The young lady told my friend that she read her welcome email from the CEO and noticed all my friend's accomplishments since the time she had worked there before. She was thoroughly impressed. She had been saying that she wanted to return to school, but she just didn't have the confidence or the motivation, until my friend encouraged her.

Amazing! Even your personal best can encourage and motivate others to get moving. You never know who is watching you, and quite frankly, you shouldn't care. The only person you care about watching you is *you*! Even my friend's husband returned to school and obtained his bachelor's and master's degrees. He, too, achieved his personal best.

My friend got busy and made every moment count. She gave it all she had, and just like that, her life was changed for the better forever. She had no regrets, only satisfaction and celebration. She gave it her personal best.

The Plan

It's not enough to simply jump out there and give it all you've got. The key to success is planning and executing the plan. Speaking of planning, a dear colleague of mine, who we will call Dawn, was one of the most organized people I know. She was sharing with a few of us some simple advice that had proven to work for her. She encouraged us to write a basic business plan or outline of what we wanted to see happen in our lives. She instructed us to simply outline a few goals with a timeline, a budget, a plan of execution, a mission statement, a vision, and anticipated outcomes. She added that there was no need to spend tons of money on fancy, overpriced, hard to understand electronic business planning templates, apps, or software programs.

Please use the "Busy Planning" template below to help you get started. Simply answer as many of these questions as you can to help you get started with your *plan*!

Busy Planning Template

Picture created in 2022 and authorized by Wendy McKinney.

Please answer the questions above in a narrative form or in a list format to help guide you and help you get *busy* in creating the plan for getting it done. Oftentimes, staring at a blank canvas can influence blank thoughts. Conversely, staring at a canvas that has the beginning touches of creativity can stimulate even more creativity. Before you get it done, you have to get it started. These questions will help get the engine turning.

The Balance Beam

A word of caution: while you are busy giving it all you've got, one thing to keep in mind is balance. Balancing is tricky and can be quite challenging.

When I was a gymnast in high school, one of my favorite events was the balance beam. It was also the most difficult and the one from which you could suffer the most injuries. On the balance beam, to reach optimal performance, every move must be specific and precise. The slightest mistake can cause a concussion or a broken bone. If you watch a gymnast on the balance beam, you will notice a pause or a break for a few seconds between every move. That is what I call "freeze and squeeze"! To avoid falling off the beam after a jump or a flip, we were taught to freeze and squeeze to regain or ensure our balance. This would help us avoid what could result in a major catastrophe. One mistake could potentially bring a gymnast's routine and career to an abrupt end.

And so it is with life, the need to constantly "freeze and squeeze." In this crazy thing called life, with all its jumps, flips, and turns, we need to freeze and squeeze to help secure our balance. We need to stop and evaluate our schedules, goals, health, and family life to successfully achieve this thing called work-life balance. There's work, there's life, and then there is balance. Just like every move on the balance beam, they must be executed independently, deliberately, and precisely. The optimal scenario in both cases is to get each move to flow together in harmony.

Although each of these has many variables, work is a part of life and life is a part of work. On the balance beam, sometimes gymnasts must surrender and jump off, or dismount, because they overcompensated their last move and are way off balance. When this happens, it does not mean the routine is over. In life, this does not mean that you have been defeated. It simply means that it is time to regroup, refocus, and complete the routine with a few adjustments. You can jump back on that balance beam and finish strong. Give it all you've got, and go grab your medal!

After giving all you've got, fall out and rest easy. In other words, get some sleep! Let us end this section with a nice nap.

Wendy Freeman-McKinney circa 1983.

Busy Sleeping

> "Go to bed, you'll feel better tomorrow" is the human
> version of "Did you try turning it off and on again?"
> —Author unknown

A great way to make every moment count is to give yourself permission to rest. You need to rest to have the energy to fulfill your mission, spend time with your family, and reach your goals. Rest is more important than we realize, and most people do not get enough of it. According to the American Sleep Association, fifty to seventy million adults in the US have a sleep disorder, 48 percent reported snoring, and 37.9 percent reported unintentionally falling asleep during the day at least once in the preceding month.

Even when I was a little girl, I thought sleeping was a waste of time. I felt like I should be playing instead of sleeping. I would always think that being sent to bed was a punishment. As I grew into an adult, I continued the poor habit of not getting enough sleep. I applauded myself for being that person who could function with three to four hours of sleep. Pulling an all-nighter in college was a weekly routine. I did not realize the harm I was doing to my body. I also had no idea that my brain was suffering because of my poor sleeping habits, nor did I realize that lack of sleep was affecting my memory.

> Your future depends on your dreams, so go to sleep.
> —Mesut Barazany

I began researching the effectiveness and importance of sleep and found quite a bit of information. I put together this pneumonic tool to help us remember some key areas:

S: Sound sleep means your body is rebuilding, resulting in improved heart health, circulation, and regulated blood pressure.

L: Longer sleep means better sleep, seven to eight hours at a minimum. This is a must for successful weight loss.

E: Extra napping goes a long way! This can give you that extra push you need to reach the desired productivity level.

E: Energy comes from a good night's rest, along with improved memory, concentration, and brain function.

P: Perfect for beautiful and amazing dreams.

My husband and I both have histories of poor sleep habits, so we have established a bit of a "sleeping toolbox."

1. Take a hot bath with Epsom salt and essential oils before bedtime.
2. Turn off all the lights in the bedroom.
3. Turn off all electronic devices.
4. No electronic devices can sleep in the bed with you.
5. Eye masks can help take sleep to another level.

6. Agree to a "lights out" schedule if you have a partner.
7. Try not to fall asleep on the couch at bedtime.
8. Get dressed for bed. Put on some real pajamas.
9. Read quietly before bed. Nothing scary or stressful.
10. No water or beverages too close to bedtime.

To reach our goals and experience success, sleep must be a priority. We cannot be too busy to get some sleep. Now is the time to begin developing and embracing this new habit, if you have not done so already. We must be deliberate in our commitment to getting more rest and do whatever it takes to get the adequate sleep that our bodies require. Our bodies will thank us. Our friends and family will thank us. We will feel brand-new and equipped for achievement.

OK, now you have all you need to give it all you've got. And don't forget to fall out and rest easy!

Time for Busy Steps!

Busy Giving All You've Got

Questions & Self-Reflection

1. Describe how you will give it all you've got.

    _____

    _____

    _____

    _____

    _____

2. Describe your strategy for time management. What does a twenty-four-hour day look like for you?

    _____

    _____

    _____

    _____

    _____

3. Name a project, goal, or task you have been wanting to finish. What (or who) is holding you back?

    _____

    _____

    _____

    _____

    _____

4. What do you need to do to finish it?

    _____

    _____

    _____

    _____

    _____

5. How do you maintain balance in your life?

    _____

    _____

    _____

    _____

    _____

6. What changes can you make to help improve your sleeping habits?

    _____

    _____

    _____

    _____

    _____

Busy Getting It Done

Don't make excuses for why you can't get it done. Focus on all the reasons why you must make it happen.

—Ralph Marston

GID, SID, and START

I would like to introduce you to a few of my family members who I have grown to love and depend on. After meeting them, you will grow to love and depend on them as well. Meet the twins, Cousin GID and Cousin SID, and good old Uncle START. You are going to love them!

Are you working on your business, obtaining your degree, upgrading your weight loss program, intensifying your spiritual life, or reconciling a relationship? Whatever it is that you want to accomplish, to get it done (GID) you will have to shut it down (SID)! Whatever it takes to reach that goal, something has got to give. Something must change. Something must go! Sometimes it's someone who has to go! Sacrifices must be made. The sacrifices may be temporary or permanent, but something must go. You must create space and energy for that next opportunity, dream, or goal. If that space is occupied, then there is no room for progress. You can keep *trying* to do it, but you don't want to die trying and limit your success.

Years ago, I heard someone say you can find a lot of dreams and great ideas at the cemetery. People have died never fulfilling their dreams. Getting it done means you must START something first. You must *stop* what you are doing and *take action right then*, or you might just keep planning and wishing—hoping and dreaming—until you are physically, emotionally, mentally, financially, or spiritually unable to execute your vision. Do it now! Nike says, "Just Do It"! Art Williams of Primerica says, "Just do it! Do it! Do it!"

The kryptonite for Cousin GID and Cousin SID is that four-letter word: procrastination. Well, it is actually a fifteen-letter word, but it might as well be a four-letter word, because the consequences of procrastination, oftentimes, will make you want to swear! Procrastination is like a disease. Avoid it at every cost, if you can! It is the act or habit of procrastinating that can kill progress, especially with something requiring immediate action. Procrastination can be a pure dream killer.

On the other hand, for a very small but exceptional group, procrastination can be fuel for the fire of creativity and imagination. Those in this unique group often get their best inspiration when they are closest to their deadline. In essence, they are shutting it down and getting it done! There can be an unusual surge of adrenaline that is released after hours of thinking, doodling, drafting, and contemplating. Some of the world's greatest works have been birthed out of the souls of a world-class procrastinator. "I love deadlines," writes Douglas Adams, "I like the whooshing sound they make as they fly by."

Check out these world-class procrastinators who were some of the most accomplished human beings in the world.[2] Remember, these are the exceptions to the rule.

Mozart

Mozart was known to be a bit of a drinker and was known to have written pieces while hungover. It has been said that he wrote the overture for his famous opera *Don Giovanni* the night before it premiered, while hungover.

Leonardo da Vinci

Leonardo da Vinci often doodled for hours before he finished a painting. It would take him years just to complete one painting. It took him sixteen years to complete the famous *Mona Lisa* painting and thirteen years to complete *The Virgin of the Rocks*.

Victor Hugo

Victor Hugo's (acclaimed writer of *Les Misérables*) unique strategy wins the prize! He would take off all of his clothes and strip down naked to keep himself from going outside and procrastinating. Then he would instruct his servants to hide his clothes from him until he had met the deadlines.

Bill Clinton

The forty-second US president, Bill Clinton, is famous for being one of the worst procrastinators in the world. He would drive his staff crazy. He would keep them waiting and waiting for responses to important documents, speeches, projects, and more! *TIME* magazine even wrote an article about his infamous procrastination back in 1994.

Margaret Atwood

Margaret Atwood is author of *The Handmaid's Tale*. Although Atwood has an impressive bibliography, she has also been known to be a world-class procrastinator. Throughout her fifty years as a writer, she published fourteen novels, nine short stories, and sixteen poetry books. However, Atwood attributes her success to a simple strategy. She gets up every morning with the intention to start writing. Instead, she often procrastinates all day and ends up starting at about 3 p.m. It is at that time when she feels she can finally get focused. Sounds like this is a great strategy that has contributed to her success.

Please do not take this as a "keys to success" component. As a reminder and best practice, procrastination should be categorized as something to be avoided at all costs. As the saying goes, please do not try this at home! While these procrastination methods and styles worked for the megastars above, they all would probably agree that this may not work for everyone. They were all particularly fortunate to have staff and support to help get them through the trenches. Unless you are like one of these superstar procrastinators, waiting, wanting, wavering, wondering, wishing, wasting, and withering will get you nowhere fast!

The antidote for procrastination is to START (stop and take action right then). Once you START, you must see it through to completion. That is where shutting it down comes in. I was able to finish this chapter today because I decided to shut it down and get it done. I didn't go to church today. I didn't get my lashes done. I didn't scroll through my social media. I made a commitment to myself not to stop until I *got it done*!

Do not stop until your goal materializes. You may have to miss a birthday party, family gathering, or a night out on the town, but this is your purpose! This is your mission. The world is waiting for you! Completing that goal or dream will help you change the world! Your family is counting on you to finish. Your friends are waiting on you. You are needed. You are special. You are gifted. You are an inspiration. You are highly favored. I heard someone say, "If you do not do it, someone else will." Well, believe it! If you do not shut it down and get it done, someone else will do it for sure! To help you get started, let's explore a method called the power of one.

The Power of One

> When you're hitting a wall, focus on one brick.
> —Tyler May

"Power of One" Tips

1. Start with *one* dollar when saving money.
2. Start with *one* minute to start exercising.
3. Start with *one* task when working on a project.
4. Start with *one* page when writing your book.

Starting may seem like it can take forever. If you can accept that it only takes one minute—one moment—to be effective, it becomes easier to yield and refocus on your goal. What happens almost every time is that one minute becomes two minutes, two then becomes ten, and the next thing you know, you're on a roll. The secret is to just simply START. Success wins almost every time.

I tricked myself into a thirty-minute workout on a spin bike by committing to only one minute. I told myself I would only work out for one minute, then I would try more the next day. After I got started, I said, "I'm on here now! I might as well go a little longer." Just like that, one minute became thirty. I also tricked myself into thirty minutes of writing in my journal by committing to only one minute and one page. I ended up writing a life plan and came up with ideas for three books, a conference, a blog, a newsletter, and a radio program. My creativity was flowing. It was crazy, and so awesome, that I couldn't stop. Whatever it is you aspire to achieve, try starting with *one*. What is the one thing you can do to help you get started?

Equally as important is finishing what you start. By any means necessary, no matter what, whatever it takes, you must finish! Like starting a painting on a blank canvas, with one stroke, the color will speak to you. Writing one word to start a song, essay, or idea, one word will speak back to you! Just see it to the end.

Unfortunately, finishing can be easier said than done. In some cases we will need to redefine the meaning of the word "finish" to help us actually reach completion. Here are a few framing alternatives.

1. Letting It Go

If you are a perfectionist, try your best to let it go and allow yourself to make some mistakes. Accept the fact that you may make a few errors. Just get it done. You can make corrections later. If you hold on to the mind of a perfectionist, your definition of "finish" might cause your project or task to never materialize.

2. Life Is a Draft

I heard someone once say, "Life is a draft!" That really stuck with me. What a great way to view your task or project to help you reach completion. What a great way to redefine "finish." If you consider your finished product a draft, subconsciously or consciously, you can push through to the finish line, knowing that at some point you can always return to, add to, enhance, or change it later.

3. Imagine, Visualize, or Meditate

We discussed this one in another chapter, but I think it's worth repeating. Imagine, visualize, or meditate on the anticipated outcome. Enjoy the moment of actually seeing the completion of the project or task. Write down the expected outcome on a poster board or a sticky note that you can look at every day. Draw a picture of it. Record the details of your visualized outcome on some sort of device so that you can play the narrative back, over and over again, until it becomes real to you. Fantasize about the results and the impact it will make on others. This exercise can possibly motivate you toward completion. As I am anticipating the completion of this book, I have envisioned the box of finished copies arriving at my door. I am visualizing the first book signing in my friend's backyard, by her pool, just like she promised. I can clearly recall the dream I had with Oprah sitting next to me at a book signing that is super crowded, with a line that has no end. I can see the workshops, the conferences, and the presentations packed with supporters and advocates. I can imagine the testimonials of how the concepts and tools helped so many people. These thoughts and pictures in my mind are pushing me to the finish line. Try it! It really works. I can actually feel the energy building inside me, granting me just enough motivation to finish! Oh, what a feeling!

Let's explore another success strategy to help get things done. This is going to be good! Jump in!

ECDC (Eliminate. Consolidate. Delegate. Create.)

A UCLA college professor once told me, if you want something done, ask a busy person to do it. It took me about ten years to understand what that meant. I always felt like a busy person never had time to get much done because they were just too busy. I eventually realized that the busy person the UCLA professor was referring to, in her profound example, was the busy person who was productive and had systems and effective protocols in place that would help them execute with precision and consistency.

She compared this person to someone who was not busy or productive, who had a lot of time on their hands, with very few commitments and limited involvement outside of their daily routines. This non-busy person would often procrastinate because they had a false sense of time and delivery of the designated task, activity, or project. The non-busy person can be seen as one who perpetuates, in their mind, the perception that they have plenty of time, when time is continuously slipping away from them, moment by moment.

In contrast, the busy productive person makes every moment count by creating and implementing every available strategy necessary to capture each phase and accomplish goals. This professor helped me to understand that, with the right approach, one can complete multiple tasks in less time. With the right systems in place, one can execute more of these tasks or activities with less effort, yielding higher-quality results.

Let's examine an effective strategy of the busy productive person called ECDC. This strategy will help demonstrate how the busy productive person gets things done!

Eliminate, consolidate, delegate, and create!

Mary—a wife, mother of three, corporate executive, ministry leader, and community volunteer—leads a busy life with many projects, goals, and deadlines. She also aims to spend time with her friends and carve out time for self-care. How does she manage to get it all done and still have time for herself? She eliminates, consolidates, delegates, and uses her creativity to get the outcomes she wants.

Let's explore the components of ECDC.

Eliminate

To eliminate in this case means to carry a lighter load! Some things you just need to get rid of. Some serious decisions must be made. What is the most important thing you need to do in that moment? *Realize and prioritize.* In other words, if you want greatness, success, accomplishments, and completion of tasks, you must begin to *eliminate.* A friend of mine said, "Success does not come without a certain level of selfishness." As harsh as it may sound, in our scenario, as mentioned in other sections, Mary might have to sacrifice relationships and miss out on especially important family events, birthday celebrations, or less urgent deadlines in order to accomplish her goals. Mary likely attends many meetings and events. Her strategy to eliminate will involve her leaving early from the event. She might not connect with everyone and might miss some of the event. It's alright to do a drive-by! Elected officials do it successfully all the time. Sometimes they make fifteen to twenty appearances in one day. Make your visit quick, but make your visit count! People are touched by the fact that someone as busy as you thought enough of them to stop by the wedding, the housewarming party, the hospital, or to the meeting.

People might feel that Mary has blown them off or that she is being rude or inconsiderate when she only *eliminates* to make room to do what she was put on this Earth to do. Fortunately, eliminating does not have to be forever. Eliminating can be temporary. It can be a temporary deferral. In most cases you can get back to it or make up for it in another way. People usually will not understand, but once you complete that task successfully—finish writing that song, earning your advanced degree, starting a thriving business, or mastering a beautiful piece of art—everyone will begin to understand and they'll ask, "How did you do that? When did you have time?" You will say (inside your head), *I eliminated wasting time with you.* Just kidding. That was not nice! Busy doing what? Eliminating, consolidating, delegating, and creating.

Mary often asks herself these three questions when considering a decision to eliminate.

1. Does this get me closer to my goal or purpose?
2. Is my life enhanced by my participation?
3. Is there an alternative method or option that requires less time and resources?

Successful execution of the elimination strategy not only involves limiting meetings, events, and activities but also eliminating the following ten things.

1. Clutter
2. Fear
3. FOMO (fear of missing out)
4. Unsupportive friends or family
5. Worry
6. Listening to what others are saying about you
7. Self-pity
8. Bad habits

9. Negative thoughts
10. Distractions

Consolidate

Consolidate suggests that you merge and multitask or creatively combine projects with an activity, with an event, with a visit, or with whatever conflicting activity you have that needs attention. For example, our friend Mary is too busy to work out. Impossible! A finance executive from my past, who we will call Tom, was that best example of consolidating and multitasking. On a regular basis he would check in and follow up. Most of the time he would make the check-in call while working out on the treadmill. He would consolidate his daily workout with his telephone calls and meetings. This was true and genuine relationship building. He made everyone feel like a million bucks when he would call. We all knew how busy he was. He was known as the Follow-Up King. No matter who called him, no matter when they called him, he would be sure to follow up right away. *Consolidate*!

Another example of using the *consolidate* component of the ECDC strategy: For many years, early in my professional career, I used to wonder how busy, high-powered, C-level executives had time to serve on multiple boards and committees and volunteer for charitable events. Their days, evenings, and weekends were already overflowing with meetings, events, and projects. I soon realized that not only are they usually genuinely interested in the cause or the organization, but their board membership serves multiple purposes. The potential opportunities presented are endless. There are often lifelong relationships formed, significant moneymaking opportunities discovered, and fascinating entertainment perks available that these executives would otherwise never have time for.

I met a high-powered CEO of a hugely successful organization who had served on the symphony board for years. I could not figure it out until he shared with me his passion for playing the classical oboe. With his busy career and schedule, he had no time for what he really loved until he joined the symphony board. He looked forward to the monthly meetings simply because they gave him the opportunity to revisit that experience of entering the symphony lobby and anticipating the sonata. For my friend in this illustration, required board meetings included attending concerts and performances. He met the musicians and like-minded board members. The strategy to consolidate his love for music and commitment to service worked out tremendously in this case, and in others.

Delegate

I want to introduce you to Lisa (I'm protecting her real name), who shared her delegation strategy with a group of us at a conference. We were amazed by what we heard.

Here it is:

Lisa had designated twelve friends to be responsible for helping her with her daughter. She was incredibly busy running a remarkably successful business. She managed several high-profile, successful clients. Her life was filled with late-night dinners and meetings, bicoastal travel, sleepless nights, reports, edits, sessions, and more. A busy life. What about her children? What about her husband? What about herself? There is no easy answer, but delegating and using the ECDC strategy helped quite a bit.

Regarding her young daughter, twelve friends agreed to help her with different areas of her daughter's life so that her daughter, Tiffany, would not miss out on some of the most important and significant events and activities in her life. One friend was delegated the responsibility of checking in on her educational needs such as school projects, teacher meetings, school assemblies, project selection, and execution. Another friend was delegated the responsibility to be her stylist; she would take her shopping, to hair appointments, to select her wardrobe, and more. The third friend was delegated the responsibility to be Tiffany's athletic coach. She agreed to take her to sports practices and games, follow up on sports activity needs, make uniform purchases and selections, and make sports activity decisions or changes. Friend number four was responsible for other extracurricular activities like dance class, music rehearsals, play dates, etc. You get the picture. Lisa was amazing at delegating, clearly. Lisa was unusual and unique because who even has an inventory of twelve friends who will commit to helping your children and basically step in for everything? Not many. However, Lisa delegated *and* got creative and found a way, and it worked!

Create

In this chapter, to *create* means to use nontraditional methods and strategies to achieve a goal that, to most people, appears impossible. In other words, find a way and make it work. Our friend Lisa, in our previous example, was an expert delegator, but she was also especially creative. She needed help with her daughter, and she got creative and found a way.

My former CEO, Eli Broad of Kaufman and Broad Inc. and SunAmerica financial services, became one of America's largest and fastest homebuilders after he decided to get creative and borrow twelve thousand dollars from his in-laws to help him get started. He was a young accountant, early in his career and newly married. He noticed how his tax clients were making tons of money in real estate. He wanted to take care of his new family and build his business, so he got creative and followed his plan. First, he borrowed the money because he didn't have any. That's creative financing at its best. Next, he found a business partner who knew more about the business than he did: class A creative collaboration. Finally, he bought and built homes that were unique. To lower construction costs, he got creative and eliminated the expense of building a basement and added a carport instead. He sold sixteen houses in one weekend. In two years, he sold six hundred homes. That is what I call creative genius.

ECDC has successfully worked for many, and it can potentially work for you to help you achieve your goals and reach your dreams. You deserve it. You are worthy of it, and the world welcomes your greatness. Again, this is not a one-size-fits-all solution, but hopefully, there are nuggets that you can preserve and apply to your circumstances.

Talk! Talk! Talk! Talk!
—Edna from The Incredibles

> Don't talk, just act! Don't say, just show!
> Don't promise, just prove!
> —Hiroko Tscuchmoto

Shutting it down and getting it done means doing and not talking. Following through with a vision is so important. Things may not end up exactly as you had planned, but if you follow through, it is a guarantee that you will get closer to your goal.

Sometimes people are satisfied with just talking about a plan or idea as if that is as good as actually executing the plan. Well, talking about the plan just isn't good enough. There comes a point in time when it would be best if you would stop talking about it and sit down and get busy doing it.

The energy you use talking about the plan or idea can take the place of the energy you need to accomplish your goal, leaving a deficit in your ability to perform or move forward. It is up to you. It is a simple decision. For the sake of everyone's peace of mind, you should probably make the decision that you are not going to be satisfied with just talking! If you decide to *do* then there's nothing more to say except: "I'm finished!" "I did it!" "We did it!" "God did it!" "It's done!" "Thank God!" "What's next?"

There was a distinguished character in the award-winning, computer-animated superhero film, *The Incredibles*, produced by Pixar Animation Studios. Edna was known for her signature line, "Talk! Talk! Talk! Talk!" Edna would repeat that phrase and abruptly interrupt someone when she felt they were babbling unnecessarily, as she had no time for that.

I had a good friend in college who reminded me of the talker that Edna, in *The Incredibles*, was often referring to. My friend, who we will call Talking Tina (not the one from Rod Serling's *The Twilight Zone*), was quite the talker. As a matter of fact, it was probably what I enjoyed most when hanging out with her. When it was time to study, we would go to the library together. We would unload our heavy backpacks that were filled with oversized textbooks, college-ruled spiral notebooks, assorted neon highlighters, mechanical pencils, and an HP 12C financial calculator. We shared the same major, economics. We were ready for the study session of a lifetime. Talking Tina was not quite ready. Talking Tina would spend the entire duration of our four- to six-hour study session talking about her plan for studying. She would create grids and graphs. They would be color coded on poster boards and note cards. She had everything organized in perfectly labeled file folders. Talking Tina presented the best study plan with time blocks and alarms. You could not lose with her study tips and tools. The problem was that Talking Tina only talked about what she was going to do, but she never actually did it. As a matter of fact, Talking Tina talked herself right out of college before graduation.

Fast forward thirty years. I am proud to say that Talking Tina's award-winning graphs and grids finally paid off. Talking Tina is now Dr. Tina, lead professor of education for a university. It was her season to bloom. I am so glad Dr. Tina finally stopped talking, shut it down, got started, got busy, and got it all done!

Haters, like parrots, talk much but cannot fly. Dreamers,
like eagles, say nothing but conquer the skies.
—Matshona Dhliwayo

Wendy L. McKinney

The *Cult of Done Manifesto*[3]
(By Bre Pettis and Kio Stark)

And finally, the manifesto of getting it done!

The *Cult of Done Manifesto* offers thirteen principles for *getting things done*. The list is unique and idiosyncratic. One might find the list useful for helping to avoid procrastination and perfectionism. I chose four of my favorite principles to share with you.

1. Accept that everything is a draft. It helps to get it done.
2. There is no editing stage.
3. Pretending you know what you are doing is almost the same as knowing what you are doing, so just accept that you know what you're doing, even if you don't, and do it.
4. Laugh at perfection. It is boring and keeps you from being done.

Before you procrastinate, begin. Before you begin, plan.
Before you plan, visualize. Before you visualize, dream.
—Matshona Dhliwayo

Time for Busy Steps!

Busy Getting It Done

Questions & Self-Reflection

1. Which of these three family members would be the most important to help you attain success, and why? (Cousin SID, Cousin GID, or Uncle START.)

    _____

    _____

    _____

    _____

    _____

2. When evaluating the power of one, can you identify the one activity, task, or project that you need help with getting started? What is the one thing that you can do?

    _____

    _____

    _____

    _____

    _____

3. Which component of ECDC has worked for you, and why? If none of them, which one would you like to implement?

    _____

    _____

    _____

    _____

4. Are you a talker or a doer? Is there something you are talking about that you should be executing instead? What is it, and how will you change to execution?

_____

_____

_____

_____

_____

5. What does the *Cult of Done Manifesto* say about perfection?

_____

_____

_____

_____

_____

Busy Saying No

Focus does not mean saying yes, it means saying no.
—Steve Jobs

Very successful people say no to almost everything.
—Warren Buffett

There are *many* ways to say *no*! Need some ideas? Here you go! Practice these words and phrases in the mirror (with no responses).

1. No, no, no, no, no!
2. I'm not available.
3. I have another commitment.
4. I won't be available, but I know someone who could come in my place.
5. My son/daughter is performing.
6. I have another engagement.
7. I will not be able to participate/attend this time.
8. I would love to, but maybe another time.
9. I'm sorry, I won't be able to.
10. No, I really cannot make it this time.
11. I cannot.
12. Thank you, but I cannot.

13. I have a scheduling conflict.
14. Unfortunately, I will be out of town.
15. It is my birthday/anniversary/Groundhog Day/me day!
16. I have to work.
17. Thanks for thinking of me, but I will not be able to this time.
18. I have an appointment.
19. No, thanks. I will pass.
20. I am moving this week.
21. I have to wash my hair.
22. No, thank you! I'm full. I have had plenty.
23. No, thank you! I have had enough.
24. No, thank you. I don't want anymore.
25. No, I will have to think about it.
26. Not now, but maybe another time.
27. No, not at this time.
28. I am going to have to pass on this one.
29. No, thank you. I'm really not interested.
30. No, thank you. I'm good.

One of the most important words that one must master to ensure success and make every moment count is the word *no*. Surprisingly, that word means the same thing in many languages. The word that often gets us in trouble is a kinder, gentler word. It is easy to say. It rolls right off our lips. People love hearing it. It is often a relief when you say it, even if you should not be saying it. That word, of course, is yes.

Saying *no* can appear selfish, coldhearted, and mean when you are really, very simply put, trying to make every moment count.

Busy doing what? If we said yes to everyone who asked us to do something, go somewhere, or give them something, we would have little time to do anything for ourselves. There are people who waste their lives away by saying yes to everyone and no to themselves. If you remain busy making every moment count for everyone else, you will miss out entirely on the great things in life for yourself.

What Can Saying No Do for You?

- Saying *no* can extend your life. It can give you power. It can help create time and space for creativity and purpose.
- Saying *no* can help relieve stress and release endorphins.
- Saying *no* can help you shed pounds.
- Saying *no* can get you higher compensation.
- Saying *no* can strengthen a relationship.
- Saying *no* is simply exercising discipline.
- Saying *no* can help grow your savings.
- Saying *no* can help you obtain wealth.
- Saying *no* can save a marriage.
- Saying *no* can break an addiction.
- Saying *no* can improve your health.
- Saying *no* can help save precious time.

Saying *no* can be easy for some but the most difficult thing in the world for others. Those who have difficulty must practice saying *no* as if it were a speech or presentation that they were preparing for, until they are comfortable with the concept and the word begins to flow without thought.

How to Balance a "No"-Centered Life

Here are four steps on how to balance a "no"-centered life without losing all your friends, family, and significant relationships:

1. Always offer an alternative.
2. Be extremely sensitive of your tone.
3. Provide as much of an explanation as you can, but try not to talk too much.
4. Share the specific benefit of saying *no* or the consequence of not saying *no*, when appropriate.

Always Offer an Alternative

In other words, if someone asks you to join them on an outing or to attend an event, you might ask them for the date of the next event or outing and offer to possibly attend that one instead.

Another example might be if someone asks you to participate in an event, like leading a presentation or filling the last seat for a group event that requires a specific number, you might suggest another participant. Maybe you can call the person you are suggesting ahead of time, before you respond, and make sure they are available. This at least will help to provide a solution, instead of leaving your requestor completely hanging.

This way, *no* does not mean *no*. Instead, your response sounds more like, "Here's another option, idea, or plan." You will appear more supportive and concerned instead of apathetic or indifferent. The best part is that you can now use your time to concentrate on something you would rather do or really need to do. Maybe you just do not want to go or participate at all, and that is OK too! This is your life. These are your moments. You get to decide. You get to choose. You own your time and your space. You do not have to share it unless you want to. It is up to you. It is a great relief to own your time. You will be moving that much closer to your purpose or beyond what you ever imagined. Maybe you will finally get some well-deserved rest or time to meditate and focus. Ah, this sounds refreshing and amazing to me in this very moment! It is amazing to see what offering an alternative will do, if you just say *no*.

Be Extremely Sensitive of Your Tone

Honestly, it is truly how you say it, and not really what you say! The examples above suggest a variety of methods for how to say no in the most sensitive way possible. If your tone is too abrupt or direct, it can seem rude and thoughtless.

However, if you take your time, think about your response for a second or two, and then respond, the outcome might be better received. Keep in mind that your goal is not to harm or offend, but to simply connect and convey something different than what your requestor had in mind.

For example, if you are involved in a discussion regarding your compensation for a new job or business contract, instead of responding immediately by saying something like, "No way, that is not enough!" or by putting a frown on your face or showing shock or disbelief, you might pause. Allow for quiet space to enter the conversation, give it some thought, and respond with something like, "I'm sorry, that is not the offer I was expecting. Thank you for your time." Or, "Thank you for the offer. However, I would like to ask for ..." Again, remember, it is the tone, not necessarily the words. In this case, it is about your livelihood, so a careful response is essential.

Provide as Much of an Explanation as You Can, but Try Not to Talk Too Much

Here is an example. Maybe your decision to say no has to do with the fact that you are not feeling well, but you do not want to go into the details. You can simply say that you are not feeling well. You don't have to say, "I woke up this morning with the worst stomach cramps and couldn't get out of bed. I haven't been able to eat a thing and I just couldn't keep anything down." Then, later that evening, they see you throwing back shots of tequila and spicy chicken wings at a birthday party on social media. Now you are backed into a corner, obligated to explain. If you keep it as simple as, "I am not feeling well," that could mean you felt better later and you were well enough to muster up the strength to get your partying on. It happens.

The truth of the matter is that it really is not anyone's business why you have decided to say no to the invitation to the baby shower or no to the offer of a tasty desert or no to that tempting job offer that really takes you off focus. Sometimes you just do not want to say yes. Guess what! You do not have to. I had a family member who consistently replied to unwanted invitations with this question, "What's the date again?" and "What time does it start?" but she would never say yea or nay. That response was one of the most strategic and effective responses I had ever heard. Most everyone fell for it time and time again, without even knowing that she had absolutely no intention of saying yes, not for one second! Just genius!

Oftentimes, you might try to explain the reason or reasons for why you have to say no, and the listener begins to read all sorts of pointless, useless, incorrect, or misguided messages, making a bigger mess than ever. It is almost always best to keep it simple, short, and sweet. Less is definitely more in this case. My mother often quoted, "Let your words be few and seasoned with grace!" Now, that is a winner. There are some cases where you might have to go into more detail than other times, but the rule of thumb is still to say as little as possible. The listener will ask you questions for clarification if they feel the need. You can guarantee that. Fortunately, most people will take what you say at face value and keep it pushing.

Share the Specific Benefit of Saying *No* or the Consequence of Not saying *No*, When Appropriate

One specific area where most people have challenges saying no is in the area relating to food. For some reason, people just do not want to let you off the hook if you say no to a savory appetizer or to a decadent desert, even if you explain that you are on a diet or you are giving up carbs and sugar. Somehow, they think you are behaving arrogantly or in a condescending manner when you are merely trying to exercise a tiny bit of discipline. When you say no, the person offering says, "Oh, come on! Just take a tiny bite. One little bite won't hurt you!"

When you continue to say no, they sometimes become belligerent and irritated, and may even attack you. "What's the matter? Are you on some crazy crash diet or something?" You want to reply with, "Yes, I am, and you should be on one too, based on that seemingly sizable Michelin tire of a waistline you are showcasing!" Oops! Sorry. That was not nice. I had a flashback!

I am ready for this one. I received some advice for this one some time ago. Here is a great response for the aggressive party host who is offended by your rejection of her handmade, gourmet tray pass. "I will have to say no, because of health reasons." For some reason, this one works 100 percent of the time. She will not accept a plain, old, nicely spoken, "No, thank you." However, a slight mention of a possible near-death illness will get them off your back every time. It is unfortunate that you must go to such great lengths, but sometimes your no must be strategic to be effective. Saying *no* for the benefit of saving your health is extremely appropriate and important in this case, and in most every case.

Sharing the consequences of not saying *no* can also be equally as important. For example, someone invites you to a dinner party where you will have the opportunity to network with several potential major business contacts. Unfortunately, you are unavailable because you are in school, seeking a specific certification, and have a number of assignments with pressing deadlines. Of course, meeting those potential business contacts would be great and could change the course of your business. However, the consequences of saying yes outweigh the former. The consequences of saying yes could result in not completing your class, not receiving your certification, and not being selected for the new multimillion-dollar contract, for which the certification is a required prerequisite.

There may be times like these when sharing a little more detail might be important to help maintain the relationship, so that the requestor understands your sincerity and commitment. Most people should understand how important it would be to say no in this case. Avoiding those consequences resulting from not saying no will keep you unnecessarily busy.

The "No" Profiles

There are several different types of "no" profiles. Let's discuss four. Which one sounds most like you?

1. The "Extreme No" Profile

Let us call him Edward the Extreme. Edward was a dedicated, committed, and disciplined bodybuilder, among other things. He was definitely an overachiever in every way, in almost every area of his life. Everything he did pointed him toward reaching those amazing "stretch" goals in his life. He said *no* to everything and everyone that was not directly aligned with his professional, personal, financial, spiritual, or academic goals, to the point of oftentimes appearing rude and selfish. However, he was (and still is, many years later) as fit as a professional athlete and has achieved many accomplishments in many areas of his life. Although his approach to *"no"* seems to be extreme, he appears to be quite happy and content with all that life has brought him. I'm not sure how many relationships he sacrificed or opportunities he missed out on, but his method seemed to work for him.

The one recommendation to offer Edward comes from number two of the four steps on how to balance a no-centered life: be extremely sensitive of your tone. It wasn't necessarily what Edward said that was not the most effective, but it was how he said no that may have cost him a few relationships. Exercising step two might help Edward keep a few life-enhancing relationships.

2. The "Never Say No" Profile

Let us call her Nancy, Who Never Says No. Nancy is a leader in her community and is exceptionally talented and well-liked. She says yes to appointments, yes to travel, yes to business meetings, yes to counseling sessions, yes to parties, yes to speaking engagements, yes to breakfast meetings, lunch meetings, and dinner meetings. She says yes before the invitation or request is completely given. She says yes to the idea of a request. We wouldn't call her a people pleaser. She simply wants to help and support as many people as possible in their endeavors and goals. She wants to make sure she is always available and never misses an opportunity to help. It is her calling and her gift.

OK, maybe she is somewhat of a people pleaser, but not in a bad way. Oftentimes, she finds herself being guilty of becoming a bit of a "sandwich maker." "Sandwich making" occurs when one commits to multiple requests or events at the same time, with several different people or organizations. Our friend Nancy often finds herself making sandwich appointments. We might find that Nancy will double-, triple-, and even sometimes quadruple-book her appointments, leaving very few avenues on how to coordinate or get out of them. Her assistant makes appointments for her to keep her on track, only to find that there are other appointments that are being confirmed at the same time. Her assistant will ask her, "Did you make another sandwich today?"

While Nancy considers herself to be fulfilled by remaining terribly busy, there is definitely an opportunity for streamlining.

Injecting a few *Busy Doing What?* strategies might help Nancy improve upon making every moment count. ECDC (in a previous chapter) is an example. While Nancy has no shortage of relationships, other areas in her life could likely use a little more attention to help her more effectively make every moment count.

3. The "Terrified of Saying NO" Profile

Let us call this one Terry the Terrified! Terry the Terrified can also be known as the "No" Chicken. She literally becomes sick to her stomach when she has to say no. For her, having to say no is like the feeling one gets when stepping off the platform to bungee jump. Having to say no is like the feeling of being locked in a cage with a den of lions and tigers. Having to say no, according to Terry the Terrified, is like the feeling you get when you are slowly approaching the first dip on a roller coaster and you wish you had taken the chicken exit when you had the chance. Terry is not like Nancy, who just does not like to say no. Terry is terrified of saying no!

Terry is so terrified that she will attend multiple events on the same day, that started at the same time, that are located in several different places, just to avoid the sick feeling of having to say no. She feels as if saying no suggests some type of weakness. Saying yes to everyone and everything reveals a sort of superpower for her. When she says yes and avoids saying no, she envisions herself becoming stronger, like Wonder Woman. Is Terry afraid to say no because she sincerely wants to support everyone and everything? Is she afraid to say no because she is afraid she will lose friends and associates? Is she afraid to say no because she thinks she will be all alone? Is she afraid to say no because it reminds her of a terrible experience from her past? The answer is, all of the above.

Terry is one of the kindest people on the planet. She is loved by many and has no shortage of friends. However, Terry is experiencing some sort of struggle and suffers from the "disease to please." Terry's behavior and her responses to others could indicate that she battles with insecurities and low self-esteem. These insecurities can be personal, professional, or relational. This is common and human nature. Once Terry comes to the realization that saying *no* is actually good for her health, her fear might gradually dissipate. When Terry says *no* to others, she opens opportunities for self-care and more time for herself and her family. Saying yes to everyone is not sustainable and can cause elevated stress and burnout. When Terry says *no* to others, she says yes to her goals and her purpose.

I am not a licensed therapist or psychologist, but while discussing Terry's actions with a licensed therapist, he indicated that Terry the Terrified might benefit from reaching out for support. The anxiety brought about by this fear could potentially pose a health risk.

A suggested strategy that is readily available for Terry would be practicing the thirty ways to say *no* that are listed at the beginning of the chapter. Take it slow, but start saying *no*! While this isn't a guaranteed fix, it will hopefully help Terry gain confidence in saying no, enhance her health, and reduce some of her anxiety.

Here are a few more nuggets that might help Terry with her fears.

- Love and accept who you are.
- Be comfortable being uncomfortable.
- Shut those negative thoughts down with inspiring "I am" statements.

- Accept that you will make mistakes.
- Look at past failures and experiences as lessons and opportunities.
- Focus on professional development and improvement.
- Practice those thirty "no" statements!

4. The "Perfect Balance of No" Profile

Let us call her Perfect Patty! Perfect Patty offers one of the best balances of no. She is really a "no" expert! She has even managed to master saying no with a huge smile on her face every time. Somehow, when Perfect Patty says no to someone, she makes them want to support her *no* in every way. She says no with a smile, as if she really would say yes if she could, and that she wants to say yes. She is dying to yes. She would give anything to say yes, but she just cannot say yes at this time.

Perfect Patty makes it appear as if she has bent over backward and tried to do everything she could to make a yes work, but it just couldn't happen this time. Her smile is so huge and so genuine when she says no, you do not want to question her or ask her why. You want to rearrange everything just to accommodate her. You wonder, *Where is that smile coming from? Can I get one of those when I say no?*

There is something very genuine about Perfect Patty's no. When she says no, it appears to come from a place of passion and love, never to manipulate or deceive. One thing for certain is that Perfect Patty is quite the planner. She plans, makes a commitment, and keeps it no matter what. Perfect Patty skillfully makes time for herself, her family, her business, and her community. Somehow, she manages to get it all in. When scheduling a meeting with

Perfect Patty, she might have to schedule it several months out, but you can rest assured that she will keep that commitment. There will have to be a major emergency for her to cancel. As a matter of fact, Perfect Patty almost never cancels.

While Perfect Patty is incredibly involved with her family and community and makes time for herself, we notice that Perfect Patty manages to keep her life as simple as possible. She tends to stay away from complicated situations and convoluted circumstances. Perfect Patty has managed the art of saying no, with the perfect balance of when to say yes! Is Patty perfect? She certainly sounds like it. Of course not, no human being is perfect. Some work harder or smarter at reaching their goals. I am sure there are many things Perfect Patty would like to improve upon. Her approach to saying no is a great example from which to learn.

Be Sure to Be Busy Saying No to the Overs!

Let's Meet the Overs

Has there ever been a time when you were terribly busy being overwhelmed, overworked, overspent, or even overcommitted? As we evaluate our approach and strategy for making every moment count, by learning to say no we must include committing our efforts toward avoiding the Overs. Have you ever met the Over family? If you haven't, we will meet some of them in a moment. They are quite the family that you will never forget.

All the members of the Over family are not bad, but there are quite a few of them that you may want to avoid, especially when you are striving to do your best to stay *busy*, making every moment count. Here is a list of my favorite Overs to avoid. Have fun and pick your top five. That is, select the top five to which you want to say *no* but are currently experiencing a struggle.

Let's start the introductions.

THE OVERS

Overwhelmed
Overeating
Overspending
Overexerting
Overcommitting
Overworking
Overthinking
Overmedicating
Oversimplifying
Overstimulating
Oversubscribing
Overemphasizing
Oversleeping
Over exaggerating
Overinvesting
Overprotecting
Overprescribing
Overpersuading
Overcomplicating

Overdecorating
Overregulating
Oversaturating
Overdramatizing
Overgeneralizing
Overadvertising
Overestimating
Overindulging
Overcrowding
Overcharging
Overdressing
Overcooking
Overshadowing
Overstressing
Overburdening
Overextending
Overbuying
Oversexing
Overdrinking
Overtalking
Overdoing
Oversleeping
Overstaying
Overheating

Picture created in 2022 and authorized by Wendy McKinney.

Over-Steps: Admit, Ask Why, and Replace

- First step to saying *no* to the Overs is to *admit* that you have an "over" issue.
- Second step to saying *no* to the Overs is to find out *why* you are overdoing it.
- Third step is to find a *replacement* for the "over" issue.

For example, if your "over" issue is overeating, first admit that overeating is a real concern for you. The second step says to identify why. Maybe you are too busy to prepare healthy meals or to stop and eat a healthy breakfast or lunch. Maybe your schedule is just too busy. Maybe you are stressed out about something. Maybe you are eating for comfort to cover another issue. Once you have identified why, it is time to move on to step three.

The third step is to find a replacement for the "over" issue. In this example, it is time to "freeze" and "squeeze." It is time to stop and take action right then (START). It is crucial that you stop and create a plan of attack. It is time to readjust your schedule, start meal prepping, drink more water, order from a meal prep service, sign up for some physical activities, or whatever the plan is to replace the "over" issue. The Overs must be replaced as soon as possible to help speed up the process of making every moment count.

*Over*view (ha ha) of how to say no to the Overs:

1. Admit
2. Ask why
3. Replace

As easy as 1-2-3 (Well … sort of!)

Time for Busy Steps!

Busy Saying No

Questions & Self-Reflection

1. List your three favorite "no" responses (i.e., "I won't be able to make it," "I have another commitment," etc.)

   1) _____
   2) _____
   3) _____

2. List the four steps to balancing a "no"-centered life.

   1) _____
   2) _____
   3) _____
   4) _____

3. Which "no" profile most resembles you, and why?
   ☐ Edward the Extreme
   ☐ Nancy, Who Never Says No
   ☐ Terry the Terrified
   ☐ Perfect Patty

   _____
   _____
   _____

4. List the top four Overs that you struggle with and how you will get *over* them!

1) _____

2) _____

3) _____

4) _____

5. What are the three easy steps to saying no to the Overs?

1) _____

2) _____

3) _____

Busy Living, Loving, and Laughing

Fight less, cuddle more. Demand less, serve more. Text less, talk more. Criticize less, compliment more. Stress less, laugh more. Worry less, pray more. With each new day, find new ways to love each other even more.

—Dave Willis

Living, loving, and laughing. These three jewels should be cherished like the precious gems that they are! Busy living means to STOP the business of life and enjoy every moment to the fullest. Busy loving means to connect without judgment and to forgive unconditionally. Busy laughing means to push past the pain and celebrate!

Busy Living

If you are not present in the moment, you will miss the moment. If you miss the moment, you are moving through life without fully living. Busy living means to:

- See the opportunities present (STOP).

- See the opportunities present (STOP) and enjoy every moment.
- See the opportunities present (STOP) because we don't know how much time we have.
- See the opportunities present (STOP) because we don't know how long our loved ones will be around.
- See the opportunities present (STOP) and put worries aside.
- See the opportunities present (STOP) and have a blast.
- See the opportunities present (STOP) and be positive and encouraging to others.
- See the opportunities present (STOP) and do what you love and what makes you feel free.
- See the opportunities present (STOP) and *live*!

Busy living means doing what drives you and not what others drive you to do. Busy living means living your life and not someone else's. Busy living doesn't mean winning every race or reaching every goal, but enjoying the journey, every step of the way. Busy living is turning off your phone when your spouse is sharing the details of their day. Busy living is pausing and applauding someone for a great accomplishment. Busy living is pushing past your fears and singing karaoke on stage, zip-lining for the first time, or going back to finish college after decades. Busy living is stopping and taking notice of the flowers, trees, sunshine, and the rain. When I was in college at UCLA, I had a geography professor who would regularly remind us to walk often and take notice of the beauty around us. He said when we are speeding by in cars, we miss the beauty of our environment. We miss the melodies created by singing birds. We miss the romance of the amazing but fleeting sunset. We miss the picturesque transformations of the autumn trees. Busy living is creating wonderful memories that will last a lifetime. Busy living is not dwelling on the past or planning the future; it's making every moment count.

Live a stress-free life ... as stress-free as you can make it. Try to keep things simple. It will reduce the number of burdens you have to carry. Decide to live. Choose to live! Live because you can. Live because you are alive!

Life is a beach! Believe enjoyment always can happen. Although we have responsibilities like work, bills, taking care of loved ones, and eating healthy, life should be enjoyable. You only get one here on Earth (that I know of).

I heard a famous Irish toast from Kevin Hart (my amazing former boss). He said, "I would like to make a toast to lying, stealing, cheating, and drinking. If you must lie, lie with the one you love. If you must steal, please steal my sorrows. If you must cheat, cheat death because I would not want to live a day without you. If you must drink, drink in the moments that take your breath away."

My mom died at age fifty-seven of breast cancer. She never saw me get married. I cried all the way down the aisle. She never saw my dress. She never went with me to the tasting, to choose flowers, or to decide on the guest list. She never met my beautiful children. I cried leaving the hospital with my first bundle of joy, bawling my eyes out because I had to accept that my mother—who was the best mom and grandmother on the planet (in my opinion)—would never meet her adorable grandchildren. They would never experience the best grandma hugs in the world. They would never taste her award-winning cooking or one-of-a-kind red velvet cake.

I remember shopping at Babies "R" Us. I was about seven or eight months pregnant, looking for new baby supplies, strollers, bedding, etc. I looked over to the next aisle and there was a young lady who was about as pregnant as I was. She had on a cute, ruffled baby doll maternity blouse with matching solid maternity stretch pants. I could see her feet swelling a little in her cute Tory Burch flats. Standing next to her, comparing strollers, was clearly the enormously proud grandmother-to-be. It was the most precious mother and daughter moment I could have ever imagined. I found myself staring, then suddenly, I became overwhelmed with sadness. The tears rolled down my cheeks right there in Babies "R" Us. At that moment I realized the harsh reality that I would never have that moment with my mother! I could not stop the tears, so I left my overstuffed basket and ran out of the store to find some secluded corner where I could scream and cry my eyes out. And I did; I cried for hours. Why am I sharing this incredibly sad story? I plead with you! Stop and live! Create memories! Do not simply cherish them, but continuously create as many as you can. Take the time! Make the time! Find the time! It is worth it! I'm sorry to be talking about death, but death unfortunately helps make life so relevant. Without death we do not realize how valuable and important life is, so stop, live, and make every moment count.

Busy Loving

Busy loving? Love yourself. Love others in spite of their faults and shortcomings. We all have faults and shortcomings. No one is perfect. Everyone deserves a pass at some point. People are usually doing the best they can with what they have. Sometimes people simply need a space to love comfortably, without judgment, and to be loved. Sometimes people do not know how to love until someone else shows them. Love is free! At least it does not cost any money, that is. Well, sometimes it can cost everything, but that info is in a different book.

Love does, however, take effort. That is for sure! Make loving a habit so it does not take so much effort. Learn to love yourself. Go easy on yourself. Forgive yourself. You are the only "you" that you have. Loving yourself makes it easier to love others. Loving yourself makes it easier for others to love you. How do you learn to love yourself? Start first by forgiving yourself and realizing you are an imperfect human being.

This famous passage always encourages me:

> Love is patient and kind. Love is not jealous or boastful or proud or rude. It does not demand its own way. It is not irritable, and it keeps no record of being wronged. Love does not rejoice about injustice but rejoices whenever the truth wins out. Love never gives up and never loses faith. Love is always hopeful and endures through every circumstance.
> —1 Corinthians 13:4-7 (New Living Translation)

I have been blessed to have a husband who, for several decades, had loved me unconditionally. In spite of my faults, shortcomings, and constant mistakes, his love for me continues. When we run into difficulties in our relationship or with life's circumstances he says, "Don't make it a big deal!" That's love. He still calls me Shaboo, the sweet nickname he gave me when we first got married.

He doesn't just say the nickname alone, he says, "my Shaboo," adding a special touch. I have no idea what it means or where the name came from, but when he says it, I just melt and I know it means "I love you." I am very fortunate that he has been patient with me over the years. I think I would have left *me* a long time ago. Thank God love is patient and love is kind. My husband also shows love by being the peacekeeper. He is the first one to apologize. I'm so grateful that he does because I am terrible at apologizing. I'm still working on that.

Love always wins. Everyone can be in different stages of love, so the best thing to do is to let people love you where they are and vice versa. Ease up on your expectations of love. Love unconditionally. Love without reservation. Love without explanation. Love without expectation. That way you never have to experience disappointment. Love and forgive. It takes the burden off of everyone and makes life sweeter.

Busy Laughing

Laughter is good for the soul! Laughter is like medicine! Laughter brings about a positive change in almost any situation. I dare you to laugh in the middle of a group of people and keep laughing. I promise you that, before long, everyone will be laughing without even having a reason. Laughter is enjoyably transmissible. Like love, laughter is free! It does not cost a thing, and it can change your current circumstances immediately. Comedy and comedians are so popular because the effects of laughter are transformational. It is so important that we take time to laugh. It is so important that we create space and opportunities for laughter. Laughter eases tension. Laughter removes stress. Laughter can extend your life. Laughter can make issues in your life seem less challenging.

Humor is infectious. The sound of roaring laughter is far more contagious than any cough, sniffle, or sneeze. When laughter is shared, it binds people together and increases happiness and intimacy.

> A joyful, cheerful heart brings healing to both
> body and soul. But the one whose heart is crushed
> struggles with sickness and depression.
> —Proverbs 17:22 (The Passion Translation)

Laughter triggers healthy physical changes in the body. Humor and laughter strengthen your immune system, boost your energy, diminish pain, and protect from the damaging effects of stress. Best of all, this priceless medicine is fun, free, and easy to use.[4]

A dear sister-friend of mine was recovering from cancer and had many nights of pain. She recommended a life-changing remedy to other patients that helped her through those painful nights … *Nick at Nite*! She said it provided some of the best laughter and healing ever. *Nick at Nite* is the late-night clean comedy segment on the Nickelodeon channel.

Several years ago I attended the funeral of a beautiful thirty-one-year-old girl who died from sickle cell anemia. To protect her identity, we will call her Jazmine. She was absolutely gorgeous and full of life when she was alive. Each person spoke of how amazing Jazmine was and of how she brightened their lives. They shared how she made them laugh. Whenever anyone would get too serious, she would do something silly to make them laugh and help ease the tension. She was diagnosed as a toddler and had been told she would not live past the age of fourteen. The song that was played during her video tribute was "Golden" by Jill Scott. Jazmine lived each day to the fullest because she was not sure if it was her last. We were told that Jazmine lived with pain every day of her life, so she was constantly reminded of her potentially shortened life span. Every photo of Jazmine filled the obituary pages with the biggest, most beautiful smile.

Looking at her photos you would never know the excruciating pain she had been experiencing. Jazmine's husband spoke so beautifully about his darling angel that God gave him on loan for a few years. He said those were the best days of his life and that they were never apart. The officiating pastor said that Jazmine's husband was chosen by God to love Jazmine as an extension of God. How beautiful!

Take one cup of love, two cups of loyalty, three cups of
forgiveness, four quarts of faith and one barrel of laughter.
Take love and loyalty and mix them thoroughly with
faith; blend with tenderness, kindness and understanding.
Add friendship and hope. Sprinkle abundantly with
laughter. Bake it with sunshine. Wrap it regularly
with lots of hugs. Serve generous helpings daily.
—Zig Ziglar

Time for Busy Steps!

Busy Living, Loving, and Laughing

Questions & Self-Reflection

1. **Busy Living:**

   If you were given the opportunity to change any one thing in your life, without any cost to you, what would you change, and why?

   _____

   _____

   _____

   _____

   _____

   _____

   _____

   _____

2. **Busy Loving:**

   What three things do you do for yourself to show that you love yourself?

   1) _____
   2) _____
   3) _____

3. Busy Laughing:

List three things that make you laugh so hard that you have tears and it makes your sides hurt.

1) _____

2) _____

3) _____

(Then think about how you can recreate that experience once a day for the rest of your life.)

Busy Living without Regrets

> Twenty years from now you will be more disappointed by the things you didn't do than by the things you did. So, throw off the bowlines. Sail away from the safe harbor. Catch the trade winds in your sails. Explore. Dream. Discover.
>
> —Mark Twain

Well, first, let us be honest. It is going to be quite difficult to get to the end of your life without regretting something. Life has its way of presenting unavoidable challenges that might come with extremely difficult recoveries. Some regrettable things that we do, we really love doing, and we do not realize the consequences until it is way past the close.

A colleague of mine shared a story about a friend who moved to Chicago to become a famous chef. He started out washing dishes at the restaurant where he hoped to become a chef. Somewhere along the way, he lost his way and forgot his dream. He never stuck to finishing his application for chef school. He thought he did not have the time or the money because life had gotten in the way. He needed to work more hours because his bills began to pile up. He had high rent, utilities, food, transportation, and entertainment expenses. Before he knew it, he was dating, then married, then had children, then medical bills, then college, and the list goes on. Twenty years went by and he was still in the same job, wishing *every day* that he had gone to chef school. Time can get away from us if we let it. We must do our best to make every moment count and try to live without regrets. I heard someone say, "It's *never* too late to become who you were meant to be!"

Please stop for a second! Plan! Take a breath! Take a train ride with a friend. Plan a trip just to think and plan! Take a sick day from work! Your health depends on it. Take a vacation day. Your life depends on it! It will be the best vacation you've ever had. Return with a new plan of attack, so you will not have to regret it later.

As I have stated before, I am not a licensed psychologist, but it does not take a license to realize that some of our end-of-life regrets come as a result of our natural inclination for pleasure. For example, people often regret not taking care of their bodies, but they had an amazing time destroying them. Of course, they did not destroy them on purpose. The destruction was slow and gradual. The destruction took years, decades. The destruction came nicely packaged with overwhelming delight and gratification. Maybe there was an occasional stomachache or a little heartburn, but nothing compared to the euphoria brought about by the biggest basket of chili con queso French fries and the largest bottomless chocolate shake that money could buy.

Another pretty common regret is having spent too many hours working. Maybe you worked too many hours each week. Maybe you never took vacations. Maybe you worked too many weekends. The correlating truth might be that you needed the income. You needed the money. Fast forward to your future. You had no idea that your spouse would divorce you because you were working so much. You had no idea that your children would despise you later in life because you were never home or at their games or activities. You had no idea that you would have so many things to regret. You were simply doing what you believed to be the right thing at the time. You thought you were doing the best you could by helping to keep a roof over their heads, food on the table, and an occasional trip to Hawaii or Las Vegas.

Jim Brown summarized this nicely in his poem, Interview with God:

> Man ... because he sacrifices his health in order to make money.
>
> Then he sacrifices his money to recuperate his health. And then he is so anxious about the future that he does not enjoy the present.
>
> The result being that he does not live in the present or the future. He lives as if he is never going to die and then dies having never really lived.[5]

Hopefully, reviewing some of the most common regrets will help us make better decisions in our lives today, before it is too late.

There have been many studies that included seniors over the age of seventy, hospice patients, and the general population collectively, that were conducted to gather the responses regarding the regrets that people have at the end of their lives. Listed below are some of the most common regrets shared.

1. They wish they had not spent so many hours working.
2. They wish they had worked out their issues with a family member.
3. They wish they had traveled more.
4. They wish they had taken better care of their bodies.
5. They wish they did not care so much about what people said or thought.
6. They wish they had taken more risks in life.
7. They wish they had taken more time when selecting a spouse of life partner.
8. They wish they had been a better parent, spouse, or son/daughter.

Regret #1

They wish they had not spent so many hours working.

> You get a job, so you can afford to have a life, but
> then you spend all your time at work and end
> up with no time to live the life you're working
> for. Any questions? We need to do a better job of
> putting ourselves higher on our own 'to-do' list!
> —Michelle Obama

This is a really tough one. What is a person supposed to do? Just quit their job? You went to school so you could specialize in this area. You graduated at the top of your class. You kept getting promotion after promotion and raise after raise. You were making more money than you had ever imagined. You had no idea that you would be working seventy- hour work weeks, but that was the only way that you could keep up. You had no idea that you would be traveling thirty weeks out of the year, but that was the requirement for the job. You had not thought about the fact that you would miss special occasions and events, like birthdays, anniversaries, and weddings, but you figured it wouldn't be like this forever. Well, maybe you had an idea, but you did not think it would be a problem for you. You thought you could manage. You were hoping you were different. You believed you were "super" and could balance it all. You tried to discipline yourself, like your colleague Glenda, who consistently shut off her computer and got out of that office at 5:15 p.m. every single day. You tried and tried some more, and you just could not do it. There was always one more thing. There was always one quick meeting you had to have before wrapping things up. There was that last set of emails that you wanted to be sure to respond to before the next day's slew of new emails poured in.

The bottom line is that it is time to decide. Do you want to start living without regrets now? Do you want to start making every moment count? There is no one-size-fits-all answer here either, but here is a suggestion. Just like the quote mentioned above, one of the keys to success is not eliminating your work, but instead, setting and managing boundaries.

> Balance is not better time management, but
> better boundary management. Balance means
> making choices and enjoying those choices.
> —Betsy Jacobson

Managing your boundaries might mean having a heart-to-heart chat with your boss to let him or her know that you cannot work on Sundays, you will not travel on special occasions (with lots of notice, of course), and that you must get out of the office at a certain time each day for your health's sake.

Anna Taylor shared this appropriate quote: "Love yourself enough to set boundaries. Your time and energy are precious. You get to choose how you use it. You teach people how to treat you by deciding what you will and won't accept."

I know someone who scheduled their workout classes immediately after work to ensure that she would get out on time. You might have to coordinate pickups, cooking, homework, etc. with your spouse or partner to help with balance. If this job is not allowing you the flexibility to live your life with some sort of balance, maybe it is time to dust off the old resume and create that Indeed online profile. The decision is yours to make. Dolly Parton says, "Never get so busy making a living that you forget to make a life!"

Regret #2

They wish they had worked out their issues with a family member.

> Forgive others, not because they deserve
> forgiveness, but because you deserve peace.
> —Jonathan Lockwood Huie

Forgive and move on. People make mistakes. Forgive them. You will need someone to forgive you at some point in your life. Even if they are wrong, forgive, love, and enjoy one another, or eliminate them from your list of associates. That is OK too. Life's too short. We do not know how much time we have here. I heard someone say, "Live every day as if it were your last!"

When it comes to a family member, so many factors are involved when there is an unresolved dispute. Other family members often feel helpless or responsible but do not know how to help or support. Often, they want to choose sides but end up experiencing great conflict with their decision. When you have an unresolved dispute or conflict with a family member, it weighs heavily on you emotionally, physically, and psychologically. It can also cause health problems. It is best for all parties involved to resolve the dispute as soon as possible. It does not mean that you must become best buds with the family member and hang out every day, but you want to resolve the conflict, ask for forgiveness, and keep the peace. You may not ever agree, and that is OK. Resolving the conflict might result in all of you agreeing to disagree. The key here is peace and forgiveness.

> Forgiveness doesn't excuse their behavior. Forgiveness prevents their behavior from destroying your heart.
> —Author unknown

It may be difficult, but do everything you can to stay focused on your mission. Life, by design, contains distractions, diversions, obstacles, setbacks, interruptions, curves, surprises, and lifestyle changes. *Find a way!* Shake it off and get back on task. The world is *waiting* on you! If you knew how much you were needed, you would press your way through the challenges and get to the success. Easier said than done? Absolutely! If it were that simple, everyone would be successful at forgiveness.

Forgiveness is an important aspect of moving forward and experiencing healing from previous hurts and pain. It is often difficult to do and can involve a slow process … The negative consequences of not forgiving has been documented in studies that show that it can lead to emotional pain of anger, hate, hurt, resentment, bitterness and so on and as a consequence can create health issues, affect relationships and stop us from experiencing the freedom that forgiveness enables.
—Ivette Moutzouris, The Resilience Center

Regret #3

They wish they had traveled more.

If you never go, you will never know!
—Author unknown

I have a dear friend who made traveling a priority for her and for her children. As a college professor, she was always teaching. She believed the best history lessons for her children took place at the actual locations where the events happened. By the time her children were barely in high school she had taken them to over thirty countries. She introduced them to unique cultures and religions. She invited them to try the most exotic foods and delicacies of the lands. They even met government officials, including prime ministers. She was determined to never allow excuses to deter her from traveling all over the world. Sometimes she even included her parents and siblings so everyone would have their own personal, life-changing experiences through travel.

How could she afford it, you ask? She and her husband saved money specifically for travel. They created a travel savings fund. They were not wealthy. She was a professor at a community college and her husband was a real estate agent. They found a way. They made it work. She found deals and planned early. She used points and any discounts she could find. She connected with travel groups and educational programs for travel. She cut back on frivolous expenses whenever she could. They reduced their cable bill, did not eat out as often, got rid of an expensive car loan, and used any other cost-saving financial strategies they could find.

Where did she find the time? She planned some trips years in advance. When it came to planning their trips during the school year, she took the children out of school to accommodate for a three- to four-week trip. Of course, she made sure to consult with all the teachers and administrators and took school packets on every trip. Each day, the children would take a break and would do homework for several hours. They would take advantage of all the great lessons from being up close and personal to the community, the residents, and the culture of the country they were visiting. They would take tons of photos and videos to create a digital diary of their remarkable travel experiences. They would create their own extra-credit projects by writing reports on the culture and current events of the area. They would study and prepare ahead of the trip, then incorporate preplanned lessons to get the most out of their travel.

I had another colleague who took a part-time job working for the airlines, just for the travel benefits. This enabled him and his family to travel all over the world for the cost of a train ride, or sometimes, practically for free. They made it a point to travel as much as possible, especially on special occasions. Dinner in Paris for their anniversary was never a second thought. A weekend in China created a great memory, although the plane ride might have felt longer than their stay. A dream trip to Europe was a wonderful graduation present, better than a car, watch, or the latest and greatest device by Apple. You can get those anytime.

> The only trip that you will regret will be
> the one that you don't take.
> —Author unknown

Regret #4

They wish they had taken better care of their bodies.

> You either suffer the pain of discipline or you
> suffer the pain of regret. Pick a side.
> —Jim Rohn

We talked about this a little at the beginning of the chapter. The bottom line here is discipline. Again, just like with most regrets that you would like to live without, it is up to you to decide whether to act or react. Most people try to take care of their body by jumping on fad diets and trying to maneuver quick weight-loss methods. This is not taking care of your body. This is essentially wrecking your body. Most ladies I know, like me, are serial dieters. It is just what we do. We see the bodies on TV, in magazines, on runways, and on social media, and we want them instantly. I am not sure how to say this, but I will say it anyway … *diets do not work*. I take that back. Diets work, as a temporary fix, if you want to fit in that dress that is two sizes too small for your cousin's wedding in six weeks. Then back up you go, go, go. Diets work temporarily, but we are talking about taking care of your body. We are talking about taking care of your entire temple. We are not just talking about weight loss here. We are also talking about your whole being. What about your mental health, which affects your physical health, which affects your spiritual health, and so on and so on?

> It is health that is real wealth and
> not pieces of gold and silver.
> —Mahatma Gandhi

Obesity is one of the most prevalent diseases in the world. Most Americans are obese and do not even know it. It seems like we have more diets available to us than there are pebbles of sand on the beach, but most of us realize that diets do not work. Trust me. I have tried quite a few of them and I know you probably have too.

There are hundreds of diets and there are new diets introduced all the time. There are liquid diets, meatless diets, starvation diets, blood type diets, lemonade diets, cookie diets, sleepless diets, and the list goes on. How can anyone ever keep up? There are apps, webinars, Zoom meetings, support groups, and still over half of the adults in America are overweight. In the United States, 36.5 percent of adults are obese. Another 32.5 percent of American adults are overweight. In all, more than two-thirds of adults in the United States are overweight or obese.[6]

A dear colleague of mine said she is a firm believer in the "no diet" diet! That is the only diet that works consistently and long-term. She says constantly, "If diets work, why is Oprah fat?" Great question. I did some research and found the top thirty-five diets. Yes, the top thirty-five, and there are eight different categories: Best Diet Overall, Best Plant-Based Diet, Best Fast Weight-Loss Diet, Best Heart-Healthy Diet, Best Diabetes Diet, Best Diet for Healthy Eating, and Easiest Diet to Follow. It is virtually impossible to keep up. How about there is nothing easy to follow here? I think I am getting stressed just by talking about this.

It really is not just about diets. It is not even just about food. What is important is achieving overall health and wellness which includes our mind, body, and soul. What about being mindful of our mental health, spiritual health, and financial health? Any breakdown in any combination of these can contribute considerably to an unhealthy body.

The conclusion is truly about deciding. No! It is not easy. It will probably be the most difficult thing that you will do in your life, but it is worth every effort. Wellness and mindfulness may come easy to some, but not for most. Some of us are seriously suffering from addictions. We may have an addiction to food, alcohol, drugs, sex, stressful circumstances, drama in our lives, or abusive relationships to name a few. Many of us need the help of a professional, and that is OK.

There are so many resources to help us eat better, sleep better, feel better, and live better.

The link between mind, body and soul is a scientific fact. We need to look after our mental health to maintain focus and clarity of the mind. It is important to develop positive relationships and genuine connection to nourish our spiritual and emotional health.[7]

I have been on a weight loss journey my entire life. It wasn't until I tore my ACL and meniscus, while beating a younger woman in a box jump contest, that I realized that moderation in everything is best. Also, that which works for others just might not work for you.

While lying in bed, having to ice and elevate my knee every day for almost a year, I thought, *There must be another way.* I had lost an amazing fifty pounds and I was quickly on my way back to finding them. I could not work out, and my meal prepping and low-carb eating plan had gone out the window. After giving myself a break, getting some rest, and focusing on recovery, I began to do my research to find out what worked best for me. I soon realized there was no perfect diet for me because my body was constantly changing and adjusting with age. However, there were great eating plans that were perfect for me. These reasonable and easy eating plans helped me reach and stay at a healthy weight while managing my glucose levels and heart health. I invested in healthy food options. I regularly met with a health coach. I learned about macronutrients and micronutrients. I did my own research. I tracked my food, water, and physical activity. I became totally committed to staying fit. I made a decision, and that's what it took. I did not penalize myself for eating an occasional Krispy Kreme donut or buffalo chicken wing order from the Cheesecake Factory (some of my favorite vices!). I measured and balanced, from week to week and month to month. If I decided to indulge, I knew I would have to pay. Sometimes I would have to adjust my nutrition and physical activity plans for weeks before getting back on track. However long it would take, however much I had to endure, I decided to give it all I had and then rest easy. I made it a point to incentivize myself for doing great, and trust me, I loved being incentivized. Did I already say that I met regularly with a coach? I maintained a host of accountability partners. I kept up with nutrition education. You must do what works for you. You must commit to being fit! Often, you will have to call for the twins, SID and GID, to help you get over the hurdles. (That is, shut it down and get it done, from the previous chapters.) It is totally up to you. The best solution is to put in the work, do the research, find the program that works for you, find an accountability partner, and make it happen!

> Almost everything will work again, if you unplug
> it for a few minutes, including you!
> —Anne Lamott

Regret #5

They wish they did not care so much about what people said or thought.

> Most people barely know themselves, so what
> does it matter what they think of you.
> —Jim Store

Unfortunately, some people have experienced so much hurt and disappointment that they struggle to be happy for themselves or anyone else. They live in a life filled with projection. They want to project their feelings of inadequacy onto you so that they can feel better about themselves. They often use damaging words and odd behaviors to try to kill your dreams. When someone is trying to kill your dreams or discourage you from pursuing your goals and plans, please remember the following.

Oprah Winfrey is one of the most successful television talk show hosts and one of the wealthiest women in the world. When she first started in the entertainment industry, she was told that she would never be successful on television if she didn't have surgery. As a matter of fact, she was fired. The producers told her that her eyes were too far apart, her nose was too wide, and her hair was too thick. Thank goodness Oprah didn't listen to any of those producers because she is worth billions today.

Walt Disney was also fired and told he "lacked imagination and had no good ideas." Industry leaders laughed at the idea of Snow White. Thank goodness Walt Disney didn't listen to the painful words and thoughts of the critics and the naysayers who incessantly attacked his ideas and creativity. The Walt Disney Company became one of the largest media companies in the world, and Walt Disney still holds the record for the most Academy Award wins ever.

Thomas Edison was one of the most successful inventors of all time. His teacher told him he was not smart enough to learn anything. If he had listened to her, we might be limited to living by candlelight and never experiencing a motion picture. Edison developed more than one thousand patents and invented life-changing devices, like the phonograph, practical electrical lamp, and movie camera.

> I have not failed. I've just found ten
> thousand ways that won't work.
> —Thomas Edison

Regret #6

They wish they had taken more risks in life.

> If you do not go after what you want,
> you'll never have it. If you don't ask, the
> answer will always be no. If you do not step
> forward, you're always in the same place.
> —Nora Roberts

Sometimes you have to just show up! Do not miss out on an opportunity. You will find out the details when you get there! You do not have to know *everything* ahead of time. Everything is not always going to come to you neatly wrapped in a package. Jobs, opportunities, connections, ideas, relationships, money, career choices, business decisions, etc. may not always come knocking at your door. Sometimes, to move forward or to get to the next level, even to a small step, you just need to *show up*! Often, we don't have the answers or a clear understanding of the outcome of a career decision, a speaking engagement, a personal introduction, a blind date, meeting with a family member, an audition, or an interview.

Sometimes you must get dressed and show up. I once knew a young lady who wanted to pursue a real estate business. Let us call her Real Estate Renee. After years of being interested in the industry, Renee finally decided to take the exam and get her license. She did not know what to do next. There were no designated work hours of eight to five that she had to report. There was no boss calling her and saying, "Where are you?" or, "Are you coming to work today?" There was not a clearly defined, paid, six-week training class. After receiving her license, Renee was on her own. There were resources, help aids, and people to talk to at the agency, but she did not know who or where or how until she decided to get dressed and *show up*!

Well, it went like this. Renee got dressed and began canvassing her neighborhood. One door at a time, she knocked and knocked until she memorized her sixty-second elevator speech. She fumbled, she misspoke, she even gave incorrect info at times. She didn't mind risking that she might be ridiculed and rejected and have doors slammed in her face. After one hundred doors, she became an expert. She gained contacts and referrals that she never dreamed of having. She just showed up. She connected with other agents along the way who became lifelong colleagues and partners. She remained consistent. Renee never quit. Her showing up became more organized and deliberate, more structured and goal-oriented. It became a systematic, sales-winning technique that she eventually shared with others.

My sister Muriel, one of the best chefs in the world, always wanted to open a restaurant. She is known for her mouthwatering barbecued beef brisket, among other delicious menu items. The preparation process for her irresistible brisket takes three whole days. People travel from all over the country to partake in this delectable delight. One day she decided she was going to take a risk and open a restaurant. She didn't have all the money she needed, but a building became available and she jumped right on it. She opened the restaurant with just enough chairs and tables and all the food supplies she could afford. She soon found out that restaurants are one of the most difficult types of businesses to maintain. After several struggling months she decided to close the restaurant and cut her losses early. After a few years she tried it again. She refused to live with the regret of not giving it another try. Unfortunately, the overwhelming requirements and responsibilities for achieving success while owning a restaurant forced her to close once again. Although Muriel was disappointed and suffered quite a few losses, this did not stop her passion for cooking. Her fine cuisine continued to be in great demand, so she quickly shifted her business model to catering and has had years of much success. Not only is her passion being fulfilled, along with lots of hungry bellies, but she is forever free of any painful regrets of never attempting to start a restaurant.

You may run across an article online, in the paper, or in a magazine, with an event related to your interest. Get busy and show up! Take a risk! Get dressed and show up! You can do a little research and background checking, but do not spend too much time on it. You might talk yourself out of it and miss out on tons of connections and opportunities. Go with expectancy. Expect knowledge, a connection, a clue, a contact, or some guidance. I promise you will leave there smarter and wiser than when you came. Get busy and just show up. Be committed to showing up! Be consistent with showing up. Be confident! You have nothing to lose but *everything* to gain. This might be risky, but you will avoid regrets. You will not ever have to say that you didn't give it a try.

Regret #7

They wish they had taken more time when selecting a spouse or life partner.

> Relationships end, but they don't end your life.
> —Steve Martin

I met a woman who was an interior decorator and a wedding planner. She was one of the most well-dressed, well-spoken, all-around talented people that you would meet. She was beautiful, kind, and fun to be around. She was a wife of thirty years and a proud mother of two. Let us call her Mary, to protect her identity. While visiting with Mary after doing some shopping for a wedding she was coordinating, Mary wanted to share something private with me about her marriage. I was eager to hear this fascinating news as my husband and I have counseled married and engaged couples for years and were constantly looking for tips, tools, and ideas. For some reason, Mary seemed especially anxious about sharing this information with me.

I saw a family photo on her mantle, and I commented on how perfect her family was. Mary turned to me slowly and looked me straight in my eyes before pausing and said, "I have been miserable for thirty years." I was in total shock. I could not believe what I thought I had heard. Her husband was in the other room, just a few feet away. In total disbelief, I asked Mary if she would kindly repeat herself, because I was sure she did not say what I thought she had. Mary kindly did repeat herself. "I have been miserable for thirty years."

She went on to explain that she knew on her wedding day that it was a mistake to get married, but she just did not have the courage to cancel everything. There had been money spent, dresses designed, caterers confirmed, flowers arranged, and family members on their way who had traveled from all over the country. She thought, *What am I supposed to do?* Consequently, Mary said "I do" and then wished for an "undo" for thirty years. I asked her if her husband knew how she felt. She said that he had known how she felt for an exceptionally long time. I asked her why she stayed in the marriage.

Her response was that he was genuinely a nice man, a good father, and a good provider. She loved him but was not in love with him. She did not want to create any instability for her children. She had thought she would grow to fall in love with him eventually, but it never happened. I asked her why he stayed in the marriage. She answered with these shocking words that left me speechless: he told her he did not want a divorce because he did not want to die alone.

Life is too short to live in misery when there is a way out. Mary sacrificed most of her life while suffering in silence. Be careful to watch for the signs when making a decision that will affect your entire life. The signs are there. When you see them, run for the hills. If you are meant to be together with that partner, waiting for a confirmation in your heart is worth the wait. You have your whole life to live. You have your whole life to be together. Try to make sure that you live your whole life with the right person. Forever is an exceptionally long time, and it is even longer when you are miserable.

Fortunately, Mary built up the courage to escape her miserable marriage and finally found and married her soul mate. Although she was a lot older, she has had the time of her life. She says that God redeemed the time for her and made time stand still.

Regret #8

They wish they had been a better parent, spouse, or son/daughter.

> To be a good parent, you need to take care of
> yourself so that you can have the physical and
> emotional energy to take care of your family.
> —Michelle Obama

Well, there are no rules or laws for being a good parent, spouse, or child. Yes, there are plenty of books with tips and suggestions. Actually, the Hebrew Bible is pretty clear with instructions about all three. Unfortunately, no one is perfect and the path for understanding each of these roles is truly trial and error.

As a parent, you may not have had the best examples and you might find yourself unconsciously mimicking bad behaviors. This can be the same with learning how to be a good spouse. If you come from parents who were divorced, you might be more of an expert in divorce than marriage, by default. Go easy on yourself. It is not easy being the best parent or spouse. It takes work and commitment.

As a child, you are evolving into who you are to become. You are a product of your circumstances and your environment. The best way to make up for not being the best child is to build a better adult relationship with your parents, if they are still around. Hopefully, you have identified the challenges now that you are an adult. This is a good time to ask for forgiveness and to do what it takes to reconcile. The best thing is to grab as many relationship tools as you can along the way. Seek counseling. Read books. Consult a friend. Attend seminars. Do whatever you have to do to make the best of your situation. Remember, it is up to you to make every moment count. You must do the work. No one is going to force you to be better at anything. You are the CEO of your own life. You make all the final decisions.

Here are my personal top ten "relationship rules" for long-lasting results. I believe these rules apply to helping keep any relationship intact, including parents, spouses, and children.

1. Forgive.
2. Be patient with one another.
3. Don't make everything a big deal.
4. Try seeing things from their perspective.
5. Highlight the other person's strengths at every opportunity.
6. Eliminate negative talk altogether.
7. Try to see the best in the other person.
8. Try to be their number one cheerleader.
9. Create a safe and loving environment.
10. Before responding during a tense conversation, *count to ten* (silently).

> Be the one who nurtures and builds. Be the
> one who has an understanding and a forgiving
> heart, one who looks for the best in people.
> Leave people better than you found them.
> —Marvin J. Ashton

In the next chapter we will provide tools and tips for better parenting.

Time for Busy Steps!

Busy Living without Regrets

Questions & Self-Reflection

1. Name your biggest regret and how you can manage it before it is too late.

    _____

    _____

    _____

    _____

2. Name a risk you may or may not be willing to take but have spent some time thinking about. Write the vision of a victorious outcome to taking that risk.

    _____

    _____

    _____

    _____

3. Name a tool or strategy described in this chapter or book that can potentially help you better deal with your regrets.

    _____

    _____

    _____

    _____

Busy Parenting

I Really Do Love My Kids.

What Are Their Names Again?

> The best thing you can spend on your kids is time.
> —Arnold Glasow

The best *present* you can give your children is your *presence*! I know you have heard it before, but please be present! How about you put down your smartphone! Would it kill you to get off the phone when you are in the car for a twenty-minute ride to school or a sports event? Every moment we spend with our children and family is precious and meaningful. Every moment, lost or missed, is gone forever. Your children should be a priority. They did not ask to become your children (not usually). Whatever way they became your children, they are *your* children now. No other parent or adult has an obligation like you do to care for them, love them, teach them, train them, discipline them, encourage them, and be an example for them. If your situation or circumstance as a parent is not ideal and isn't exactly how you would dream it to be, love them the best way you can. Spend as much time with them as you can. Take interest in their interests. Applaud their successes. Affirm their good and positive efforts and behaviors. That only costs you time. Everyone has access to time in some form or fashion. You might have to be creative. Maybe you do not live in the same home, city, or state. Maybe your access is limited because of certain unfortunate circumstances. Use technology. Email them, Skype them, FaceTime them. How about a good old-fashioned letter or Hallmark card? How about cutting out something interesting that they might like from a magazine and sending it to them through Twitter, Instagram, TikTok, etc.?

If you live together, take a moment to sit with them and ask them about their day. If your schedule is crazy and you are working on a project, sit in the same room with them while they're doing their homework and you're doing your work. Jump on a video game with them for ten minutes, even if you do not know how to play. They simply enjoy your presence. You can be busy and be with your children at the same time. Talking to your children is a lost art. Talking without judging, criticizing, or directing is hard to come by. Talking and listening is good stuff! I heard someone say to parents of newborn twins, "Please spend as much time as you can with them. They are all grown-up before you know it."

We need to build our lives and our schedules so that they include our children. Whether they are infants, toddlers, teens, or adults, they need us in their lives to love, support, affirm, and encourage them. It is an old saying, but at the end of one's life, no one regrets having worked too much or made too much money but they definitely regret not having spent enough time with their family.

Get Help from Your Village

I had a dear friend who was a remarkably busy professional businesswoman who committed to spending time with my two children because she did not have any children of her own. She loved my children as though they were her own. Every other Wednesday, without fail, she would come over to visit. She lived in another city, so these visits had to be carefully planned and scheduled, almost like a business meeting. Month after month, year after year, she kept her commitment. The boys would look forward to every other Wednesday because they knew that she was coming and that it was going to be a great day. I observed how much they enjoyed her visits, but more importantly, how they felt valued and important because they had their special time and special day. Sometimes she would only spend an hour with them, sometimes longer. No matter how much time it was, they knew that some portion of the day was set aside just for them.

Tyler Tuesday

That is when I created Tyler Tuesday. After my oldest son went away to college, I found myself getting busier and busier, leaving Tyler (my younger son) alone more often than before. I have no idea why, but I think I thought I had so much more time because I only had one child at home. I remembered the designated days my friend set up for my boys and thought that would be the perfect plan for Tyler.

Tyler Tuesday is a day that was created just for my son Tyler. The rules for Tyler Tuesday were that I would devote Tuesdays to Tyler and commit to some type of activity where my focus was on Tyler and Tyler alone. What is most important is that your child has a designated time period with Mom or Dad or a guardian, all to themselves. For example, Tyler may need help on a homework project. Most days, I am way too busy. Busy doing what? Everything, other than spending time with Tyler.

Helping Tyler had to be nonnegotiable. No phones. No email. No TV, unless that was Tyler's focus. I might have even asked Tyler what he would like to do. He may have wanted to go to the bookstore to purchase a book. He may have wanted to go for a run at the park. Sometimes he just wanted to sit and talk while I listened attentively, without interruption. If you have more than one child, you will have to be creative with your time and days. Maybe your schedule will not allow you to designate an entire day or evening to one child. Maybe you will have to split up one evening for multiple children. Please keep in mind that each child deserves their own designated face time with you. This is only a suggestion. Remember that one size does *not* necessarily fit all. What might work for you might not work for someone else. Remember, these are ideas and suggestions to help you get the most out of your life and make every moment count. What are your children's names again?

Another thing that is particularly important to children is consistency. Your schedule might not be flexible enough to make it to every game, recital, or awards ceremony. However, making some type of commitment and being consistent goes a long way. For example, you might not be able to make it to all of your daughter's basketball games, but instead you make a commitment to show up for every home game. Leave some room for grace.

You still might have to miss one or two, but do the best that you can. Do not be too hard on yourself, but if you are going to break your commitment and consistency, please be sure to explain and let the child know ahead of time. There is nothing worse than a child spending the entire game or recital looking in the audience for you.

Try to help build their confidence at an early age. Help them discover their gifts and talents early so they can be nurtured and developed. Find a gift in them and start calling them the "resident expert," or whatever encouraging name or title you can think of.

For example, my son Tyler is great at computers but thinks it's no big deal. I create time for us together by asking him to help me set up things on my computer, like programs and applications. He's well-versed on the latest and greatest cell phone technology. We might just stop by the Verizon Wireless store so I can show him off and boost his confidence while creating opportunities for us to bond together. Even if your children are older it's never too late to encourage their gifts and talents and spend quality time together.

My older son Dallas is an amazing pianist and plays all types of music. I like to brag to everyone that he is the best piano player in the world, and they should invite him to play for them for an event or special occasion. When I needed entertainment for a very exclusive fundraising event, my first thought was my favorite musician. My son played several beautiful selections and impressed each of the guests. I also have a stepdaughter, Kirstien, who is a genius and has always been the smartest person in the room. I call her my bonus daughter. I like to take every opportunity I can to celebrate and encourage her as well. She continues to excel in all that she does, and she deserves to be celebrated and honored. I may not have given birth to her, but I can contribute to helping her give birth to her dreams and goals. These moments with my children not only give me a chance to spend time with them, but they also provide opportunities for me to encourage them, promote them, and help build their confidence.

Parents can be and should be the president of their child's fan club. You might be the grandparent, foster parent, uncle, stepmom, etc. Whatever your role is, that child in your life needs your encouragement and support. Without it, other distractions can take precedence and priority and cause the child to get offtrack early. Do your part. Help give the kid a good start!

Get creative as you try to engage with your child. Here are a few suggestions for free activities to do with your children.

1. Go to a museum (most museums offer a free day every week or month).
2. Visit the park and fly kites.
3. Go to the beach and build sandcastles.
4. Cook or bake with them.
5. Paint masterpiece paintings.
6. Take them to the waterfront to splash around.
7. Ride bikes on a bike path.
8. Go on a nature walk.
9. Go on a bus or trolley adventure.
10. Drive up the coast.
11. Let your kids drive you. Allow them to give blind directions and see where the journey takes you.

And here are some activities to do with your adult children.

1. Go on local trips with them.
2. Grab them for coffee or a sandwich.
3. Go with them to the gym or for a run.
4. Meditate or pray with them.
5. Take trips to the bookstore (if there are any left).
6. Take them window-shopping.
7. Go on museum visits.
8. Binge-watch Netflix or their favorite TV series with them.
9. Attend a community event or presentation.
10. Bake or cook their favorite dish with them.

Do you really love your kids? I know you do! Do they know that they are one of the most important things in your life? Do they know that you are committed to being consistent and available or at least giving it your best shot? Do they know that they are a priority? How do you show them? Busy doing what? Busy being committed and consistent with everything you've got!

Time for Busy Steps!

Busy Parenting

Questions & Self-Reflection

1. What ideas do you have for improving your presence with your child or children?

    _____

    _____

    _____

    _____

2. Who from your village can provide support for you to help you with parenting? What specific area would they provide support in (childcare, academic support, sports, the arts, etc.)?

    _____

    _____

    _____

    _____

3. What strategies would you use to incorporate your child or children into your busy life?

    _____

    _____

    _____

    _____

4. What methods would you use to help build your child's or children's confidence?

_____

_____

_____

_____

Busy Being Great

The Time to Be Great Is Now!

> Be not afraid of greatness: some men are born great, some achieve greatness and some have greatness thrust upon them.
>
> —William Shakespeare, *Twelfth Night*

When I initially think of greatness, I think of someone who has amassed a great deal of wealth or someone who stands out among their peers for some great thing they have created or accomplished. I think of kings and queens, inventors and outstanding corporate leaders. I think of Hollywood celebrities.

Then, one day, I was participating in a discussion with a few parents who were talking about their athletic children and all their great accomplishments. One of the fathers made the most profound statement about greatness that I had ever heard. He said, "Your son or daughter might be great at sports, academics, or the arts, but someone great had to have the insight, knowledge, and tenacity to get them there." The father who spoke so profoundly about greatness was explaining that ultimately someone had to be great enough to nurture their interests. It was then and there that I began to realize that greatness comes in many forms. Greatness is multifaceted and multidimensional. Everyone has some level of greatness inside of them.

That blew me away. It made me think about that hardworking single mom who was responsible for taking her record-breaking, twelve-year-old quarterback son to his football practices and games after standing on her feet and working a full day. Hopefully, she will be the one he is sure to give a shout out to as he is handed his NFL Super Bowl ring. Should she be acknowledged as a mom who represented greatness or a mom who had a son who represented greatness? Well, I think the answer is yes to both. This amazing mom most assuredly followed her passion and made sacrifices, resulting in a life fulfilled for both her and her son.

I would like to pause and define greatness as the result of someone doing something that makes someone, or something, better off than before. I believe greatness does not have to be defined by money, status, prestige, or prominence. I believe that these are products of greatness.

> The greatness of a man is not in how much wealth
> he acquires, but in his integrity and his ability
> to affect those around him positively.
> —Bob Marley

Several years ago, I watched a documentary about the Olympic gold medalist and American gymnast, Dominique Dawes. The underlying theme was about how to raise a champion. Dominique's mother knew that Dominique was someone incredibly special when she was six years old. She knew that her daughter's exceptional talent would require a different approach for her upbringing. Dominique's mother of three knew that she had one child who seemed to show exceptional talent in gymnastics. While Dominique's mom had two other children to raise, she knew she had to make significant sacrifices for Dominique. To make sure Dominique had the best coach and the best training, her mom had to make the most challenging sacrifices ever. She had to seek out every financial resource imaginable to pay the outrageous expenses for which she was not prepared. At the height of Dominique's training, her mom had to send her away to live with her coach, to ensure that she had the best possible coaching opportunities available. This was one of the most difficult experiences, and the most exciting, for the entire family.

They were a very close-knit family. The siblings were inseparable, and this move would mean that they would not see each other for months at a time. At first, Dominique was extremely lonely and homesick and she felt out of place. Her coach's family members were exceedingly kind, but they seemed to have little in common and looked quite different than Dominique. It did not take long for Dominique to begin to become comfortable in her routine and to adjust to her host family. After an unanticipated, but graceful, adjustment and transition, Dominique went on to become the first African American woman to win an individual Olympic medal in artistic gymnastics, and the first Black person of any nationality or gender to win an Olympic gold medal in gymnastics. She is also one of only three female American gymnasts, along with Muriel Grossfeld and Linda Metheny-Mulvihill, to compete in three Olympics. That is why she is affectionately known as Awesome Dawesome!

Of course, it goes without saying that Dominique's accomplishments embody greatness at its best, but what about the contributions and sacrifices made by her parents? What about her coach? Did they ever stand on the platform and receive a medal? Was there a documentary created that featured them? Would they automatically be referred to as being great? The answer is emphatically no. Greatness is defined as distinction, brilliance, excellence, and superiority, to name a few. Greatness is revealed in one's character. Dominique's parents and her coach exemplified greatness in volumes, and there are volumes of greatness in you. Your role in greatness might be in the facilitation of greatness. Your position might be as the supporter of greatness. You might not experience the celebration or notoriety of your greatness like Oprah, Mark Zuckerberg, or Jeff Bezos. There may not ever be a news article written up or a TV segment showcasing your greatness. That does not mean that you do not demonstrate greatness in many areas of your life.

There are many levels of greatness. There is unsung greatness.

- Greatness is represented by the man or woman who commits his or her life to helping people in the community to have hope when they have no belief in anything or anyone around them.
- Greatness is the woman who goes above and beyond the call of duty to satisfy a client, customer, or patient.
- Greatness is the teacher who spends that extra time with that struggling student in the evenings or on weekends, with no expectation of additional compensation or accolades.
- Greatness is that father who works multiple jobs to care for his very large family, in spite of his limitations or disabilities.

- Greatness is that pastor who saw a child drown and committed his life to working with engineers, scientists, and lawyers to help him invent a device that will save other children from that dreadful fate.

- Greatness is that individual who sees a need in their family, in the community, in their workplace, in their church, or on the street and focuses on finding a solution, without complaining or criticizing.

- Greatness is that young person who is intelligent and knowledgeable but is respectful and patient with his elders or seniors or those in authority.

- Greatness is that young lady who was diagnosed with ADHD and dyslexia, and was told she could never succeed, but she never quits. She never gives up.

- Greatness is the first responder who chose a life of sacrifice to help recover individuals and families from destruction and disaster.

- Greatness is the distinguished gentleman or gentlewoman who makes a huge mistake and publicly apologizes.

- Greatness is the young, poor child who starts a foundation to help homeless children when they themselves have lived a life of homelessness.

- Greatness is represented by the young adult social worker who has dedicated her life to helping foster children find their way because she, too, had been abandoned by her parents, struggled through foster care, was eventually adopted, and never blamed her parents.

The list can go on and on. What is most important is that you realize there is greatness in you, whether it is recognized or acknowledged. Greatness is always there. Greatness is always ready to manifest. Greatness brings results.

When I worked for the American Red Cross, each year we celebrated what was called the Real Heroes Awards Breakfast event. Among at least ten categories, individuals were honored for acts of great bravery, dedication, and service to the community. Some of the categories recognized were: Animal Welfare, Community Partner, Fire & Rescue, Good Samaritan, Gift of Life, Humanitarian, Law Enforcement, Military, and Youth Good Samaritan. The tagline often used was "celebrating ordinary people with extraordinary courage."

Many of the honorees were recognized for simply doing what they loved and doing a great job. They were not looking for accolades. Many times, the honoree was someone who was passing by and saw a need, sometimes a life-threatening urgent need, and acted on it. Every year, there were more and more nominations, but only 10 awards. Over 150 nominations would come in across all categories.

Although there were many people to be recognized, time would only allow for a fraction. All 150 nominations contained stories of greatness. Each story offered an outcome of sacrifice, bravery, or a selfless act with no desire for personal gain. When each of them was asked the question, "Do you believe you are a hero?" 100 percent of the time the answer was a resounding *no*. The common response was, "I was only doing what I believe anyone else would do in the same circumstance." These unsung heroes were busy being great.

Judge Mablean Ephriam, former celebrity judge from Fox's *Divorce Court* TV show, has always had a heart for fathers in the community. She wanted to create a way to acknowledge those fathers who went unrecognized for going above and beyond their duties as committed and active fathers to their children. She founded the HUF Awards and started it in her backyard on Father's Day many years ago. HUF stands for "honoring unsung fathers."

The event included awards and recognition for fathers and academic scholarships for the children. The winners of these awards were nominated by their children, wives, ex-wives, parents, siblings, other relatives, friends, coworkers, and anyone who admired their great qualities.

The award categories included the Living Legacy award (for the elderly father who serves as a role model), the Solo Warrior award (for the single father), the Fatherhood Forever award (for the divorced father), the Village Dad award (for the nonbiological father who stepped in), and finally, the Love Cares award (for the married father living at home.

The event began with just a few friends and family members and then grew over the years to over a thousand guests in multiple states. There were some fathers who were receiving an award for the very first time in their lives.

There is often greatness with no celebration at an awards luncheon or banquet. It is still greatness. When you learn to celebrate your own greatness, when no one is looking and no one is there to tell you how great you are, then you have arrived. This is something of which you should be proud. This probably means you did something for someone that changed their world forever, and you did it out of the kindness of your heart.

A word of caution. Some people waste their entire lives trying to live through the greatness of someone else. Often, we undervalue our greatness and define our boundaries of greatness by someone else's. This can be unproductive. We must seek out our passions, define them, and pursue them with our whole being. It is through our passions that we find peace, fulfillment, and greatness. We never want to spend a lifetime chasing someone else's dream.

We cannot all be Michelle Obama, Mother Teresa, or Melinda Gates. We have our own dreams to fulfill. We have our own passions to follow. We, too, can do something extraordinary to change the world. We may never receive recognition or an award, and we should not look for them. Remember, greatness is an expression of our character, not of our bank account.

Princess Margaret, Countess of Snowdon, struggled her entire life, knowingly living in the shadow of her sister, the queen. From the time Princess Margaret was a little girl, she coveted the role that was destined and defined for her sister from birth. Although Princess Elizabeth (at the time) was terrified of the role and felt insecure about her abilities, she was willing to take it on. Princess Margaret felt that she was more beautiful, charismatic, and much more qualified than her sister, the heir apparent. Princess Margaret's obsession with Queen Elizabeth's role and greatness led Margaret down a path of indiscretion and indecision. Princess Margaret never gave room for her own greatness. She was beautiful, charismatic, and qualified, but the role of the queen was her sister's to have. Should Margaret have given up her dream of being queen? It is OK to dream. Never give up on your dreams. However, it is even better to identify your passion and pursue it with everything you have.

If it had been meant for Princess Margaret to become queen, because of some unforeseen circumstance, it would have happened. However, instead, Margaret chose a life that was inevitably unproductive, destructive, and unbecoming. Princess Margaret died, never having fulfilled her true God-given purpose.

The journey to greatness is a process. It takes time. You must celebrate your successes along the way. There will be setbacks and roadblocks. There will be days with distractions and deterrents. You cannot give in. You must not give up! One way to stay motivated is to visualize your goals. Spend time every day reviewing some part of your goals. Put photos, notes, and messages on the wall and on the mirror pertaining to your goals and your vision for greatness. You do not have to have all the answers right now. You do not have to have a clear vision of your goals or greatness. The journey to greatness can be like putting the pieces of a puzzle together. You might have to work on it a little at a time until it is complete.

Despise not small beginnings ...
—Zechariah 4:10 (New Living Translation)

Every experience is a lesson along the way. Welcome the struggle. Make note of it and keep it moving. Overcoming each struggle represents upward movement on the rungs of life. Even if you slip and fall, you must keep climbing. The time will move with you. Time flies when you are having fun! If you quit, if you give up, you kill the dream. If you abort the journey or the assignment, *greatness* does not stand a chance. Preparation plus opportunity equals success (P+O=S). The *opportunity* is coming. Will you be ready? Will you be prepared? Embrace the lessons as they come, knowing that graduation is near.

In sales training, it is taught that a "no" gets you closer to a "yes." How will you achieve the "yes" of greatness if you quit, if you give up? Perseverance is the best answer. Do not give up until you get what is promised to you and what you are destined to do. It does not matter how long. It should not matter how much. Greatness has no expiration date. It is birthed when it is time. Greatness manifests itself at the right time, for the right person, at the right hour, in the right space.

Therefore, being busy being great should be an easy task. After all, being great means being you!

Time for Busy Steps!

Busy Being Great

Questions & Self-Reflection

1. How would you define greatness?

   _____

   _____

   _____

   _____

   _____

2. What have you done to help make someone or something better off than before?

   _____

   _____

   _____

   _____

   _____

3. What does unsung greatness mean to you?

   _____

   _____

   _____

   _____

   _____

4. What three qualities do you believe you possess that represent greatness (i.e., integrity, sacrifice, respect, perseverance, selflessness, etc.)?

_____

_____

_____

_____

_____

5. Who is someone that you believe embodies greatness, and why?

_____

_____

_____

_____

_____

Busy Concluding

I f you believe or agree with anything that has been stated in this book and there is something that resonates with you, it is time for action. There are probably some immediate changes and adjustments that you want to make in your life. Remember, this book is not a one-size-fits-all answer to helping solve all the problems in your life. It is merely designed to help you take a step back and evaluate what is really going on in your busy life. Many of us have entirely too much busyness in our lives. Every single moment expended is gone forever. Making every moment count will require strategy, discipline, commitment, and patience. I would hope that you would agree that we must own the responsibility of making every moment count. We must be willing to do the work. It is up to us, and we must decide.

We will have busy days in our lives that may feel like we are out of control, but there are several tools and steps mentioned in this book to at least get you started with a few ideas. You might even feel like you are too busy to start planning, correcting, and adjusting your life. I hope that some of the morsels you have received will catch up to you and help you along the way. However, I promise you that there is at least one nugget in these pages that will help you get some of the life back that might have been lost because you were just too busy.

Our first chapter, Busy Prioritizing, charged us to get busy and start prioritizing. We met Rebecca, who was faced with a pressing decision. Life seemed so perfect, but it really was not. While Rebecca had a great job that many would covet, she was miserable. She needed to reprioritize her life. She had to find help. She needed counsel in the worst way. There are coaches, mentors, books, tapes, videos, seminars, webinars, wise friends, and other resources available. Rebecca was committed to finding a way, and she did. Rebecca did the work. Rebecca got busy. She saw a way out. Rebecca evaluated her priorities. She followed her passions and transformed her life. Within her plan she discovered how to prioritize and monetize and make every moment count in the lives of her children, her husband, and herself. She was able to earn profits that she never imagined would be possible. Rebecca got busy prioritizing and finally figured out how to be fulfilled and fed (financially fed, that is).

In chapter two we met Adam and Brian, who helped us understand that Busy Defining What's Really Important comes with significant sacrifices. Focus and discipline are an inseparable pair and are also keys to success here. Along with making difficult decisions, self-examination and execution are vital.

Making every moment count is virtually impossible when there are impeding distractions. Chapter three, Busy Avoiding Distractions, carefully walked us through the alleyways of distraction addiction. There are distractions and there are addictions. There is nothing worse than this dynamic duo, called distraction addictions, to help kill your dreams and your passion. There was also a discussion of the "one more thing" syndrome that is an unhealthy companion to the duo. Fortunately, steps and solutions were included for your survival.

Chapter four presented us with twenty-four hours to get Busy Giving All You've Got. Although it is a daily race, with major milestones and thrilling thresholds, your personal best is good enough. Making every moment count cannot be effectively executed without a well-designed plan. The Busy Planning Template, found in this chapter, provided simple questions and a concise format created to get you on your way. After "freezing and squeezing" on the balance beam, we closed this chapter with the Busy Sleeping component which opened our eyes to the all-encompassing, health-promoting benefits of a good night's rest.

Busy Getting It Done in chapter five is a family affair. You had the grand opportunity to meet the twins, GID and SID, who partner quite productively with good ole Uncle START. These unique family dynamics caused us to explore the correlation between the three suspects. GID and SID compel you to keep in mind that, in order to get it done, one must be committed to shut it down first. Soon after, the family role of Uncle START inspired one to stop and take action right then. Aligned with the final strategies of the power of one and ECDC, you, the reader, will be adequately equipped with the appropriate tools and mechanisms to conquer those unwanted dream killers that include fear of failure, loss, and rejection. It is then that you will be ready to get it done!

When no means no. It truly is how you say it, and not what you say, that matters. Chapter 6, the Busy Saying No proclamation, is as clear and direct as you can make it. There is no moving forward in any area of life without owning the power and the discipline to say no. Chapter 6 helped us develop our talking points and assisted us to carefully and effortlessly get to a "no." Chapter 6 cleverly delivered a comprehensive menu of "no" phrases that conveniently fit any scenario. Meeting the "no" profiles and the Overs was an experience to remember. I hope you enjoyed meeting them.

What is really important is chapter 7's Busy Living, Loving, and Laughing, not to be confused with the message of chapter 2 (Busy Defining What's Really Important). This chapter, more than any other, explored the depth and breadth of the sanctity of relationships. Once a life is gone, it is gone forever. We must be busy living, cherish every moment, and create memories at every opportunity. Loving and laughing are like medicine and are good for the soul. Learn to love yourself and you will become better equipped to love others. Laugh at yourself. Laugh with others. Laugh often. Laugh as if no one is watching.

Chapter 8, Busy Living without Regrets, was a showstopper! As human beings, we enjoy pleasure. We seek enjoyment and delight daily. Escaping a life of regrets can be tricky. Many studies show how we can be predictable as human beings. Some regrets come about because of seemingly inescapable addictions. Common regrets included not taking enough risks, working too much, and not traveling more. It's OK to start over sometimes. It's OK to insist on a redo! As it relates to living without regrets, making every moment count requires setting boundaries, being creative, exercising discipline, and forgiving others and yourself. The ten rules included in the chapter will hopefully help with sustaining relationships.

Chapter 9, Busy Parenting, was a reminder to all parents, guardians, grandparents, stepparents, or anyone who has the responsibility of raising a child, that our children need us more than ever. We must make time for them, nurture them, and engage with them at all costs. It is imperative that we pull from our busyness and show up in their lives. If necessary, we can consider reaching out to our villages for support. Making every moment count with our children encourages us to design creative activities, incorporate our children into our busy lives, build their confidence, and engage them frequently and consistently.

Chapter 10, our final chapter, Busy Being Great, nicely summed up our message. Greatness is not defined by wealth but is revealed in one's character. Every effort of busyness in our lives should point directly toward our greatness. Greatness can be defined as distinction, brilliance, excellence, and superiority. There are many levels, categories, and facets of greatness. It is important to note that greatness is inside all of us. A good rule is to never undervalue your greatness, nor allow it to be defined by someone else. Making every moment count, by identifying and pursuing your passion and purpose, is all the greatness you need.

> Make your vision so clear that
> your fears become irrelevant!
> —Kerwin Rae

Now is the time to pull out your laptop, iPad, notepad, scratch paper, poster board, or whatever writing mechanism works best for you, to begin the outline for the canvas of your life.

> Write the vision and make it plain
> that men would run with it.
> —Habakkuk 2:2 (New King James Version)

To figure out and understand what you really want your life to look like, we must write it out. We must write every detail, name, place, position, feeling, experience, and expectation that we want to see in our lives. How do you want to spend every moment? What do you consider to be living a fulfilled life? How do you want each day to look? How do you want each day to start? How do you want each day to end? Who do you want to spend time with? When do you want to spend time with them? Who do you *not* want to spend time with? What does happiness look like for you? What do you want to be the joy of your life?

Writing out the vision for your life creates clarity and motivation to succeed. When you have your vision defined, you have an urgency to see it come to fruition. Far too often we are too busy to take the time to really ask ourselves what we really want and wait for the answer. What we want, what we need, and what we need to do live inside of us. We can have and do whatever we desire when we focus and put our minds to it. Busyness can be an excuse. It can be a crutch keeping us as far away from success as possible. Today is the day to make every moment count. Today is the day that we commit to discarding busyness, once and for all, and embrace the garments of discipline, focus, boundaries, patience, forgiveness, creativity, hope, and self-love. It is the only way to achieve what rightfully belongs to us. You deserve time. You deserve space. You deserve a manageable pace for your life. You deserve living a life where you are fulfilled and fed. In other words, your life should be filled with joy while you have all the resources you need to help yourself and others you care about. BUSY: believing undeniably that success is yours! It is time. It is now. Let's get busy not being so busy, and make every moment count!

Abbreviations

BEACH: Believe Enjoyment Always Can Happen

BUSY: Believing Undeniably that Success is Yours

BQS: Busy Quitting Smart

ECDC: Eliminate, Consolidate, Delegate, and Create

FEAR: False Evidence Appearing Real

GID: Get It Done

SID: Shut It Down

START: Stop and Take Action Right Then

STOP: See The Opportunities Present

Endnotes

1   Doran, George; Miller, Arthur; Cunningham, James. "There's a S.M.A.R.T. way to write management goals and objectives." Management Review, November 1981.

2   Shatz, Itamar, "Famous Procrastinators." Solving Procrastination. September 2018. https://solvingprocrastination.com/famous-procrastinators/

3   Pettis, Bre and Stark, Kio, "The Cult of Done Manifesto." Medium. August 2016. https://medium.com/@bre/the-cult-of-done-manifesto-724ca1c2ff13

4   Robinson, Lawrence; Smith, Melinda, M.A., and Segal, Jeanne Ph.D. "Laughter is the best medicine." Helpguide. August 2022 https://www.helpguide.org/articles/mental-health/laughter-is-the-best-medicine.htm

5   Lachard, James J. (AKA Jim Brown). "I dreamed I had an interview with God." Omnieve. September 2016. https://omnievesolutions.com/2016/09/01/interview-with-god-by-james-j-lachard-jim-brown/

6   Holland, Kimberly and Bubnis, Daniel, M.S., NASM-CPT, NASE Level II-CSS. "Obesity Facts." Healthline, January 18, 2022. https://www.healthline.com/health/obesity-facts

7   Hunterlink Help. "Understanding the importance of mind, body and soul." Hunterlink. May 15, 2019. https://hunterlink.org.au/2019/05/15/understanding-the-importance-of-mind-body-soul/

Acknowledgments

There is an African proverb that says it takes a village to raise a child. Well, it certainly took a village to help me write this book. I am so grateful for the people in my village who never gave up on me. I am so grateful to all those who contributed in over a million ways. Writing this book was like running the Rock 'n' Roll Marathon and stopping at each mile marker for a celebration. I am thankful to my loving husband, George Anthony McKinney, for supporting me every step of the way. I appreciate my attentive children, Kirstien, Dallas, and William Tyler, for being my personal cheerleaders. I can't thank my sister Muriel Freeman enough for personally caring for me when my injuries tried to rule and stop my progress. I'm thankful to my only surviving brother, Jeffery, who authored his first book and led the way. What can I say about Rachel and Autumn who were there from the start with the living vision board on my birthday, then brought me swiftly over the finish line? Thank you to my generous Ghia who pressed pause on her busy life to help push the ball down the court. Thank you to Dr. White for encouraging me and trusting me with my first radio interview before the book was even finished. Of course, thank you to my LOL (Ladies of Leadership)—Marcia, Liz, and Sheryl—for reminding me that I could do it! Thank you to Auntie-Mom-Judge-Mablean Ephriam and my BFF, Tajamika Paxton, for always being there for whatever I needed. Thank you to the Impact Global Ministries family who prayed and encouraged me through the wilderness. I can't say thank you enough to my countless prayer partners, intercessors, professional colleagues, Rotarian brothers and sisters, Red Cross family, and fellow nonprofit leaders who contributed in their own special ways. Most importantly, I thank my heavenly Father for giving me the strength and the life to deliver this gift that was a gift to me first.